Model Railway Handboo

THOROUGHLY MODERN MODELS

2. *Modern Wagons in 4mm*

Before the AME kit emerged, the only way to a Cawood, PFA wagon was by scratchbuilding. A pair of scratchbuilt PFA wagons have benefited from Cawoods transfers from AME. Containers are assembled from 40thou machined Evergreen Styrene, the wagon underframes are soldered from brass channel and sheet. Axleguards are etched by A1-Railmatch, intended originally for their Kelleys/MOD PFA container flat wagon kits.

DEDICATION

To my Father in Law, Mr Archie Gibson
for all his kind support and encouragement.
For him, steam is still king.

By
NIGEL BURKIN

Copyright Irwell Press and Nigel Burkin
ISBN 1-871608-69-4

Glossary of Terms

Aggregates. A generic term for quarried construction materials, for example, roadstone, sand gravel, armour stone and marine dredged gravels. Not all quarried materials are aggregates, for example, Redland (formerly Steetley) quarry and processe dolofines for refractory purposes. **Air Cylinder**. Air receiving tank used as a reservoir for airbrake systems. **Air Distributor**. Device which equalises air distribution to vehicles brakes. **Axle Limit**. Maximum permitted loading of a wagon per axle. This is related to route availability. **Two axle wagon**. Generic term for a fixed wheelbase wagon with two axles, four wheels. **Airbrake pipes**. Flexible hoses which connect continuous air brake systems between wagons. Airpipes are located on the headstocks. **Tippler**. Type of wagon designed to discharge its load by side tipping of the body. **Cov-hop**. Abbreviation for Covered Hopper Wagon. **Pal-van**. Abbreviation for vans designed to carry standard pallets. **Van-wide**. Abbreviation for a van with large door openings. **Procor**. Wagon Builder originally located at Horbury, near Wakefield. **Powell Duffryn**. Wagon builder. **Flame tubes**. Tubes located in the end of bitumen tanks. They accept burners designed to reheat solidified bitumen loads. **Discharge Pipes**. Pipes located underneath tank wagons for discharging the load. **Knuckle Coupler**. Different to a buckeye coupler, this is a heavy duty coupler used on wagons operated in long block trains. Examples include British Steel owned ore tipplers and Mendip Rail operated box and hopper wagons. **'Inner' wagons**. Term for a wagon fitted with a knuckle coupler at both ends. It cannot couple to any other draw gear type, only to wagons fitted with the same. Used in block rakes. **'Outer' wagon**. Term for a wagon with a knuckle coupler at one end and conventional drawgear at the other. It is generally marshalled at the ends of block rakes to enable coupling by locomotives with conventional drawgear. **Number sequence**. Documented identification numbers allocated to all rail vehicles and recorded on TOPS. Each number is unique and grouped depending on vehicle type. **Number prefixes**. Letter codes allocated to number sequences to denote wagon ownership. **Departmental Wagons**. Service vehicles used by the service departments for engineering and other purposes. Ballast wagons are a good example. **Revenue vehicles**. Wagons used for freight traffic, owned and operated by railway companies. **Railease, Caib, Tiphook Rail, Marcroft Engineering, Tigerail, O&K**. Wagon building and maintenance companies. **Parabolic and Bruninghaus Suspensions, BSC friction Pedestal Suspension, Gloucester Floating Suspension**. Wagon suspension system for 2 axle wagons. See Chapter 2. **Compensation**. A method of making a model ride over uneven track without derailment. Compensation units keep all four wheels firmly on the rails. **'Solid' underframes**. Models built without a form of compensation to allow for uneven track. **Underframe**. Structural unit which supports the wagon structure, aka chassis. **Brake disc callipers**. Actuating device which applied the brake pads to brake discs either wheel or axle mounted. **Bogie wagon**. Vehicle fitted with separate bogies as opposed to a fixed wheelbase underframe. **PO Wagons**. Abbreviation for private owner vehicles. Operated by private companies, they are usually found in block trains and used solely for that company's freight. Examples include oil companies, quarrying and chemical companies. Unusual exceptions include wagon lessors. **Tare**. Unladen weight of wagon i.e., when empty. **Carrying Capacity**. Maximum permitted load i.e. GLW-tare = Carrying capacity. **Carkind**. Abbreviation for rail vehicle code names, especially those applied to departmental vehicles. Sometimes applied to TOPS codes too. **Class A Oils**. Petroleum products with a flash point below 23 degrees C i.e. aviation fuel, petrol and white oils. **Class B Oils**. Petroleum products with a flash point over 23 degrees C i.e. fuel oil, crude oil, black oils. **Unfinished steels**. Precisely that, slabs, blooms, etc. **Semi-finished steels**. Part processed steels i.e. special sections, coils, bars, rod and wire. **CRC**. Cold reduced coil. **HRC**. Hot rolled coil. **TOPS**. Total operations processing system. Computer system which documents each event affecting each rail vehicle. **Axleguard**. Metal plate which supports suspension and axlebox equipment. Feature of two axle wagons - a.k.a. W Iron. **Bolster**. Wooden or steel beam fitted to wagons for holding the load. Usually fitted with removal stations for securing the load. Common in steel carrying wagons.

Trade Suppliers

Appleby Model Engineering PO Box 104 WORCESTER WR5 2YZ 01905 351952 Manufacturer and supplier of complete wagon kits and components in 4 and 7mm scale. Also supplied correct paint and transfers for post 1970s wagons.

Mendip Models 29 Catherine Street Frome Somerset BA11 1DB 01373 452522 Manufacturer and supplier of detailing components and kits for modern wagons. Specialises in Mendip Rail prototypes. A well stocked model shop may be found at this address.

Fox Transfers Cranberry End Studios Old School House 12 Brougham Street Leicester LE1 2BA Tel. 0116 2626868 Waterslide transfers for almost everything from EWSR and private owner wagons to heritage wagon subjects.

HMRS Transfers 9 Park Place Worksop Notts S80 1HL For the PC range of HMRS transfers. (Press-fix type).

MJT Scale Components 41 Oak Avenue Shirley Croydon CR0 8EP Manufacturer of many useful wagon detailing parts. Respected in the hobby for a huge range of general modelling components and EMU conversion kits.

Mowbray Modern Models Cobblestones 1 Batemans Yard Market Place Thirsk North Yorks YO7 1EX Tel. 01845 525813 Modern traction and specialist equipment supplier.

Railmatch Products c/o Howes 12 Banbury Road Kidlington OXFORD OX5 2BT Tel. 01865 848000 For all Railmatch products including the A1 Models range of parts and kits. Stocks the full range of A1 Railmatch rolling stock parts. A well stocked model shop may be found at this address.

M G Sharp Models 712 Attercliffe Road SHEFFIELD S9 3RD Tel. 0114 244 0851 Leading stockist of US outline materials, decals, detailing and RTR equipment; Kadee Couplings and general models.

Shestos Unit 2 Sapcote Trading Centre 374 High Road London NW10 2DH Tel. 0181 451 6188 For tools, airbrush equipment and spares. A huge range by any standards.

Ultrascale Gear Services Letchworth The Wynd East Letchworth HERTS SG6 3EL Tel. 01462 685327 For wheel packs, wheel sets, gears etc

When writing to mail order suppliers, please remember to enclose a suitable SAE for the return of lists and catalogues - and mention this book!

First Published in the United Kingdom by
IRWELL PRESS 1998
59A, High Street, Clophill, Bedfordshire MK45 4BE
Printed in Huddersfield by The Amadeus Press

Contents

Bibliography

C R Anthony and B Rogers, *Railfreight Today*, OPC 1989, ISBN 0-86093-439-X; P Bartlett. D Larkin. T Mann. R Silsbury. A Ward, *An Illustrated History of BR Wagons Vol 1*, OPC 1985, ISBN 0-86093-230-6; G Freeman Allen, *British Railfreight Today and Tomorrow*, Janes Publishing Ltd 1984, ISBN 0-7106-0312-6; D Ratcliffe, *Modern Private Owner Wagons on BR*, Patrick Stephens Ltd 1989, ISBN 1-85260-062-4; John Dickenson and Peter Ifold, *Airbraked Series Wagon Fleet Nos 100000-990049*, South Coast Transport Publishing (1990), ISBN 1-872768-13-X; Andrew Marshall, *Private Owner Wagons Vol 1*, Metro Enterprises (1990); Andrew Marshall, *Private Owner Wagons Vol 2 Tank Wagons*, Metro Enterprises Ltd (1990), ISBN 0-947773-16-9; John Dickenson and Stewart Mott, *RIV Wagon Fleet*, South Coast Transport Publishing (1990), ISBN 1-872768-07-5; Peter Ifold and Stewart Mott, *BR Wagon Fleet Vol 5 Engineers Fleet DB970000-DB999900*, South Coast Transport Publishing (1989); Peter Ifold and John Dickenson, *Engineers Series Wagon Fleet*, South Coast Transport Publishing (1994), ISBN 1-872768-12-1.

A wonderful collection of engineers wagons including a number of Seacows built to Diagram YG500H. Nearest the camera is DB980051, a Lot 3966 wagon of diagram YG500H, built at Shildon in 1981. This represents one of the later Seacows, equipped with Y27 bogies and of welded construction. Location: Tonbridge Yard.

Preface
Wagons, why bother?

A reasonable question to ask, because your typical modern freight wagon, for all its great size and complexity, is an elusive beast. Most freight still runs between private sidings during the night, making research and photography difficult. Ready to run (rtr) manufacturers must ask the same question, because tooling models is a costly business. The investment for a large wagon is comparable to a locomotive, yet market forces dictate far lower prices for rolling stock relative to locomotives. As a result of economic constraints, commercial offerings are often simplified or based on old tooling, or are toy-like in appear-

From cursory detailing to complex rebuilding of commercial rtr models; from kit bashing to the superb bogie and underframe kits now available, there is plenty of advice and ideas about for all modern railway enthusiasts keen to make some sense of the wagon scene.

Frustrations, Pitfalls, Support, Rewards
Once you step off the well trodden ready to run path, the biggest frustration is lack of information. Lack of published drawings, lack of photographic material, lack of access to the real thing. Yes, it's a problem, enough to stop all but the most de-

The reward is satisfaction, seeing the project through to the end. Success can be a spur, and finishing one project can inspire several more. All trade support should be welcomed, because without detailing and conversion components, most of the projects in this handbook would be nearly impossible. You can support the trade, encourage them to produce more bits, more kits and develop more ideas. 'Use them or lose them' is the clarion call. As freight traffic continues its dramatic revival, the railway modeller wants to know more about freight operations, the wagons themselves and, more importantly, how to model them. Whist this

Awaiting transfers and matt varnish is my HFA model, built from spare Hornby MGR hoppers and an underframe kit from AME. Always scour the ads in magazines for handy spares.

ance. Yet the wagon is becoming the locomotive's *raison d'etre* in the 1990s. Sprinters have seen to that by replacing hundreds of locomotive-hauled coaches.

There are lots of arguments against spending valuable modelling time on them, so why bother? Fortunately, many modellers take a simple attitude; it's there, so I've got to build it! Mountain climber's syndrome, so to speak, and scratchbuilding rare prototypes becomes akin to Munroe bagging and adds spice to the hobby. Well, you don't need to go to those lengths; plenty of accessible material is available to keep you occupied in the modelling room for many a Saturday night.

Scope of the Book
The range of possible projects is huge, and the greatest difficulty I encountered was what to leave out, not what to put in. The projects selected are ones which, above all, employ general techniques, which can be applied to almost any freight vehicle.

termined modeller but if information is not immediately at hand, there are ways to get it. Pitfalls there are aplenty, but the biggest no-no is trespassing on railway property. Simply do not do it! The effort to obtain permits is well rewarded. Alternatively, target your wagon from public places, stations, public footpaths and the like. Trespassers brand every enthusiast with a bad name, making life difficult for me and others like me to obtain information and permits.

Another pitfall is 'attitude'. Many seem to think they have God-given rights to drawings and information. Not so. Make contact with relevant companies and do so with courtesy. As a final word on this subject, avoid falling into the trap of wanting measurements of every minute detail. Many are standard, and much of the work is done for you by the model trade. If you cannot find one of ten leading dimensions, then make an intelligent estimation - you are unlikely to be far out...

handbook is aimed primarily at the modern image modeller who wishes to explore the products, techniques and ideas available to build a convincing collection of wagons, there is something for almost every modeller to enjoy.

The emphasis is on stripping the mystery away from modelling modern wagons, by explaining the technologies involved, naming the parts and suggesting uses for the growing range of detailing components. Not all wagons currently found on Railtrack are featured by any means, but commonly found vehicles are described, illustrated and modelled in a simple, straightforward way.

This is a handbook for the work bench, written to inform and solve problems. I hope you have as much fun with the models as I have had writing about them.

Nigel Burkin
Pewsey November 1997

Great Rocks Junction yard is often full of vehicles used for aggregate traffic from the intense quarrying activity in the area. This is a good spot to visit with a camera. Modern wagons offer colour and variety, perhaps more (whisper it) than steam era counterparts.

CHAPTER ONE
Research

Prototype Background Information
Modern Railfreight operations have a long legacy of development, from the first standard BR wagons of the 1950s. Development was linked to increases in maximum permitted axle loading, air braking and block train working. Landmarks include:

Early 1950s: British Railways inherited a fleet of worn out former private owner (PO) and railway owned (RO) vehicles. Apart from a few specialised types, the PO wagon as such had all but disappeared.

Mid 1950s: BR standard wagons introduced, including many innovative and 'modern' vacuum braked designs. Some were derived from pre-nationalisation diagrams. The policy was to discourage PO wagon development in favour of RO general user vehicles. ie Common Carrier policy.

1957: Some PO wagon development for block train working was considered when the first 35 tonne vacuum braked tank wagon was developed for high speed, continuously braked block train workings.

1964: First 45 tonne (46 tonne) monobloc tankwagon designed with vacuum brakes for high speed operation. Monobloc designs permit larger diameter barrels, increased capacity and improved efficiency.

The design was adopted by the oil companies in large numbers.

1966: Axle loading increased from 22.5 tonnes to 25.5 tonnes on most key routes.

1970 to 1972: BR policy change; rail customers encouraged to invest in their own wagon fleets, bearing in mind the age and declining condition of the large fleets of standard vacuum braked and unfitted RO vehicles. Exceptions to this policy included general freight and traffic from nationalised industries. During this time, BR developed modern designs for coal and steel traffic. This policy remained unchanged until the sale of Trainload Freight to EWS.

1971-75: Introduction and development of TOPS (Total Operations Processing System) computer technology from the USA for efficient vehicle utilisation.

1974: Section 8 grants become widely available for PO wagons and terminal facilities.

By 1984: Speedlink network complete and fully operational after several years of development. With the odd exception, airbraking progressively replaces vacuum braked trains on revenue services.

1987: Sectorisation of Railfreight into five operating companies specialising in specific trainload freight traffics, except Railfreight Distribution.

1992: TOPS runs out of codings for PO wagons under 'P'. Codes 'K' and 'J' allocated to improve code utilisation. 'P' retained for 2/3 axle vehicles.

1992-94: Speedlink rationalised, then disbanded as a political cost cutting exercise. Railfreight concentrates on block train load traffic within sectors. Freight traffic haemorrhages as strict financial performance targets are squeezed.

1994-6: Privatisation required the reorganisation of sectors into three new companies: Loadhaul, Transrail and Mainline. Transrail Enterprise Network is established as a way to maximise resources and introduce an efficient wagon load freight system. All three freight companies (along with RES) are successfully targeted by Wisconsin Central to form English, Welsh and Scottish Railways (EWS).

1996-7: EWS turns the freight business upside down as redundant wagons are re-employed, traffic won and a revolution of the freight business commences. New locomotives and wagons are ordered. Freight revival is established. Regular freight returns to the Far North of Scotland for the first time in many years.

VNH1 bogie under PFA RLS92636. Didcot August 1997.

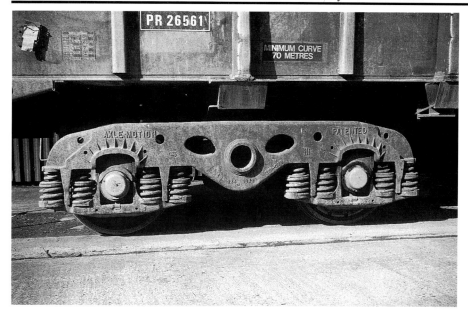

Top. BSC axle motion bogie under ex-iron ore tippler (outer) PR26561. Merehead September 1997.

Middle. Eight foot plate back bogie. Chester July 1997.

Bottom. This bogie often causes confusion with modellers who always refer to works drawings for the Salmon, which shows an 8 foot plate bogie. Wagon fittings and bogies are exchanged during the life of a vehicle. Salmon No.DB996312, Chester July 1997.

1997: EWS signs new contract with Railtrack for flat fee package to enable growth of business. Railtrack criticised for poor support of freight revival as outlined in business strategy. York works reopened for the construction of 5,000 new freight wagons.

TOPS (Total Operations Processing System)

A computerised system introduced to monitor each vehicle event, movement, availability and location. TOPS has a proven record in improving vehicle productivity. It saw the introduction of new numbering systems and wagon codes based on four letters, to replace the confusing telegraph codes. TOPS codes offer exact descriptions of each wagon type, with a unique identifying number. PO wagon operators benefited in having access to TOPS to locate their vehicles, whilst leasing companies and Railfreight could re-assign empty vehicles to traffic with minimum delay.

Private Owner vehicles numbered 1000 to 99999.

Railway owned vehicles numbered 100000 to 990049.

UIC registered vehicles retained the continental 12 figure numbers.

Number sequences are intended to keep airbrake wagons separate from older vacuum/unfitted wagon records. Prefixes are tagged onto TOPS numbers of engineering vehicles to denote operating department. Three letters are used: -DC, as in:

ADC = Director of Mechanical and Electrical Engineering
BDC = BRT
KDC = S and T
LDC = M&EE Electrification
RDC = Research
DC = General permanent way vehicles.

Private owner vehicles (there are far too many to list them all) are prefixed with letters to identify owner/operator, such as:

STS = Caib UK Ltd
SUKO = Shell UK Ltd
OK = Orenstein and Koppel AG
REDA = Redland Aggregates
TIPH = Tiphook Rail Ltd

Wagon coding to complement number sequences

TOPS code first letter: Broad vehicle classification.

Second letter: Defines exact vehicle type.

Third letter: Defines brake type.

Fourth letter: Vehicle type subdivision.

Letters are combined in any order to fit the vehicle description.

Design codes are based on letter systems in addition to TOPS coding. For operational purposes, design codes are issued with the first two letters of the TOPS code and a 3 figure serial number starting at 001, for example, HE002F. This is a **H**opper wagon, type **E**, issue **002**. The last letter, **F** denotes detail changes in an otherwise standard design.

TOPS letter codes for railway owned vehicles

First letter

B Bogie Steel
C Covered Hopper
F Flat Wagon
H Hopper Wagon
M Mineral Wagon
O Open Wagon
R Operational Wagon
S 2 axle steel
V Vans
Y Department bogie
Z 2 axle departmental

Second Letter - distinguishes between types of wagon within a group, such as:

HAA MGR Hopper
HEA Household Coal Hopper
HFA Coal Hopper with canopy

Third Letter

A Airbraked only
B Airbraked, through vacuum pipe
Q Unfitted with through air pipe
X Dual braked
V Vacuum Braked

TOPS letter codes for private owner vehicles

First/second letter

Code 'P' denotes 2/3 axle wagons
Code 'K' denotes specialised wagons
Code 'J' denotes bogie wagons other than tanks
Code 'T' denotes tank wagons
PA 2 axle covered hopper
PB 2 axle grain/lime/clay
PC 2 axle presflo
PC 2 axle powder hopper
PF 2 axle container flat
PG 2 axle aggregate/salt/sand hoppers
PH Self discharge train stock
PI Cartics
PJ 2 tier cartic vehicles, outer and inner
PK 3 axle comtic
PM 2 axle mineral
PN 2 axle open for coal/aggregates
PN 2 axle timber
PO 2 axle scrap metal box
PQ 3 axle autic vehicles
PR 2 axle china clay, curtain roof
PV 2 axle palvan, curtain sides
JA bogie covered hopper
JB Bogie covered hopper
JC Bogie presflo
JD Bogie presflo
JF Aggregate hopper, low track force bogie
JG Aggregate hopper
JH Aggregate hoppers, inners and outers
JI Covered hopper RIV registered
JJ Bogie steel
JK Low liner
JL Car carrier

Top. BSC pedestal suspension. Warrington July 1997.

Middle. Gloucester floating axle suspension is fitted to PGA No.PR14243. Note that this type of suspension is 'handed' i.e. asymmetrical.

Bottom. Obtaining suitable permits will allow you to get this close. Take lots of photographs and written records. Otherwise do not trespass. Sambre et Meuse rectangular buffer with straight shank.

Choose your wheels carefully. Wheelsets destined for O&K 25/100 bogies.

Former ODA (12t pipe wagon) No.KDC113017 TOPS coded ZDA, fitted with W irons; clasp brakes and FAT 13 suspension. The suspension was installed as part of a refurbishment programme. This is nearly the same as that fitted to refurbished 12t VEA vans.

JN *Bogie open*
JQ *Side tipping open*
JR *Aggregate box open*
JS *Steel coil, with or without hood*
JT *Iron ore tipplers*
JU *Iron stone tippler*
JV *Carflat*
JW *Palvan*
JX *Bogie scrap carrier*
JY *Open bogie*
TC *Bogie Tank 80-89.9t*
TD *Bogie tank 90-99.9t*
TE *Bogie tank over 100t*
TR *2 axle tank 20-29.9t*
TS *2 axle tank 30-39.9t*
TT *2 axle tank 40-49.9t*
TU *2 axle tank over 50t*

Third letter is issued as per railway owned vehicles to classify brake types; A for Airbrake and so on.

To make sense of the technical side of modern freight vehicles, it pays to know your TOPS and design codes. Note that the above is a guide and revisions are common, especially now EWS are turning the railfreight scene on its head.

Weights
The current maximum axle loading on Railtrack is 25.5 tonnes, allowing a maximum gross of 51 tonnes for a 2 axle wagon; 102 tonnes for a 4 axle bogie vehicle. Tare is the weight of the wagon unladen. GLW is the gross laden weight; the maximum permitted weight of vehicle plus load within axle limit.

Research
Reference to publications such as wagon listings will unearth essential information on everything from private owner vehicles to the active railway owned revenue fleet. There are a few useful publications full of excellent photographs; titles like *Rail Freight Today*, published by OPC or

An Illustrated History of BR Wagons, Part One.

A picture tells a thousand words; so a good set of photographs makes an excellent source of reference material.

Magazine articles from the modelling and prototype press offer little information on wagons, being in the main restricted to news pieces of a few paragraphs. I have gathered what little material was available over the years from magazines, compiling a scrap book of reference material to support my own photographs and notes.

Trade catalogues are as important as a library of books and collections of photographs for wagon modelling. Obtain and read catalogues from the likes of A1-Railmatch; Cambrian; Mendip Models; AME etc. to find all of the vital components and kits. Often only the availability of a set of bogies makes a project possible, for the difficult bit has been done for you. Keep in touch with the Trade, they often produce limited runs of parts and components not listed in their catalogues.

What you can do

You have located all the modelling components available and delved into the availability of kits and rtr base models. The next step is to locate information on your target project. Published photographs are not ideal on their own, unless assembling a kit. You need leading dimensions to complement photographs and sketches for scale calculations. My favoured method of finding and using leading dimensions is described below.

1. Obtain copies of the Metro Publishing directories (or similar) which list TOPS codes, number sequences, operators and details of the leading dimensions of each wagon. Bear in mind that freight vehicles are built to maximise payload, so the leading dimensions of a wagon closely mirror the loading gauge. Dimensions such as overall height; width over body; width over solebars; buffer height etc. are standard. If you take advantage of this assumption, leading dimensions may be extrapolated from loading gauge charts.

Take care to determine the difference between length over buffers from length over headstocks or embarrassing errors in your finished model will be the result. If you are lucky enough to have access to diagram books or Railfreight advertising material, dimensions may be taken from the diagrams of loading areas and load space.

2. Leading dimensions are useless without photographs, so go out and find your wagon. Modern vehicles are available to study, older vacuum braked and unfitted prototypes may be out of service, so details are only available from published sources. Modern Image modellers are fortunate to be able to find their chosen subject in use. Whether a meeting with your favourite wagon is accidental or planned, always take advantage of the opportunity, get at least a dozen close up photographs of sides/ends and details unique to that type. Take measurements if you can, concentrating on leading dimensions. Don't waste time measuring or sketching details like buffers, brake wheels or bogies. They are available as detailing components, making the information superfluous to your modelling efforts.

3. Take notes of, or photograph data panels applied to the wagon. Leading dimensions are often recorded as data panels (or lettering blocks) for operational purposes. Anything from length over buffers, headstocks, body length, bogie centres and so on is available depending on the wagon type. Recorded in millimetres or metres, this is a great way to get that all vital information. The calculations for scale are simple.

A JUA bogie iron ore tippler (inner) measures 12,497mm over headstocks.

12,497mm is 12.497 metres in length
1000mm = 1 metre = 3.28 feet
12.497m x 3.28 feet = 41 feet
41 feet x 4mm = 164mm scale length in 4mm scale.
(An interesting mix of SI and imperial measurements, but it works).

4. From photographs, sketches and measurements, draw the basic outline of the wagon onto graph paper. Add major details like ribs, chutes, doors and so on to add to the overall feel of the drawing. If the proportions do not look right, recheck your calculations and notes.

This process is important for scratchbuilding projects, serious rebuilding of rtr models and using underframe kits on which a scratchbuilt superstructure is added. Graph paper drawings become templates for cutting out the parts from styrene sheet or brass. Kit building or simple detailing of ready to run models may rely on photographs alone, but simple sketch drawings prepared in the manner above are always a great help.

Airtank and distributors detail under Iron Ore Tipper. Westbury November 1997.

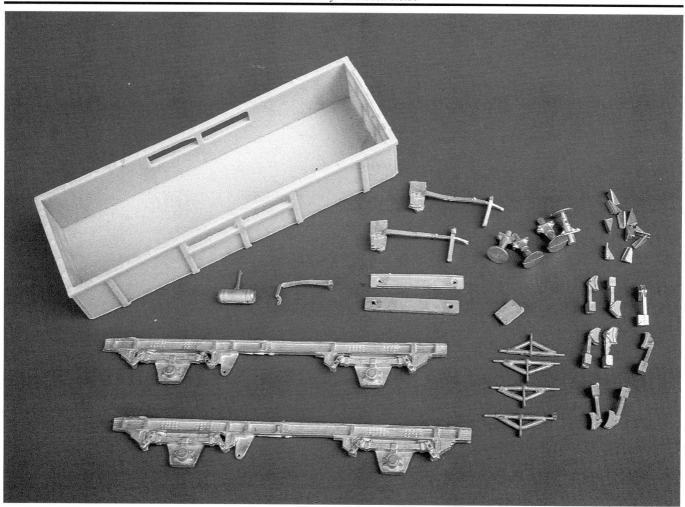

Above and below. A typical wagon list comprising cast resin body and cast white metal underframe. This is a kit from the AME range. Assembly is straight forward, using the flat base of the body to assemble underframe and MJT compensation unit.

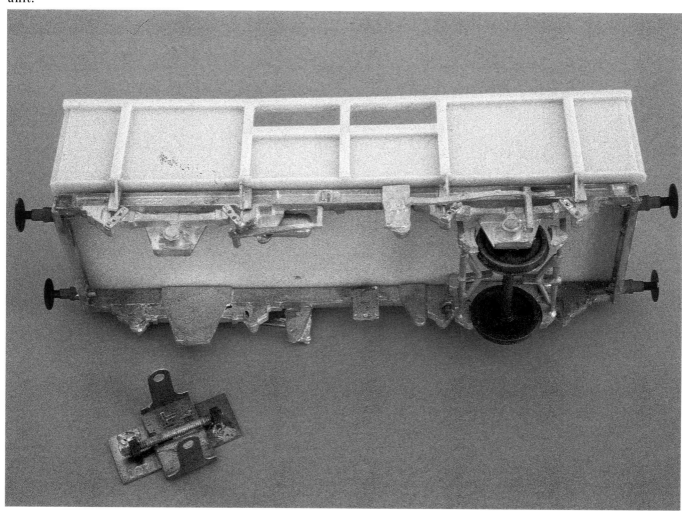

CHAPTER TWO
Getting Results.
Techniques, Materials.

All but the simplest detailing projects need a good stock of materials. A standard stock unique to your workshop develops with time but new modellers may need a guide from which a start can be made...

Polystyrene is most commonly used in injection moulded kits such as those manufactured by Ratio, Cambrian and Parkside. It is also available as a basic building material in sheets, strip, sections, tube and rod. A scratchbuilder's delight, this material is the most flexible and forgiving of all. Styrene plastic sheet possesses many attributes:

- Liquid solvent bonds it very efficiently with clean joints and no residue.
- It comes in many different thicknesses, ideal for scribing and cutting to any conceivable shape.
- It's durable and stable, and warping is avoided by the sparing use of liquid solvent adhesive and the correct use of thicker sheets for structural parts.
- Styrene will take paint and other adhesives readily without priming or other surface preparation.
- The flexibility of styrene opens many new options for modelling, not least in wagon detailing.
- It may be drilled, tapped, sanded, filed and textured with ease.

Evergreen Styrene
(Evergreen Scale Models)
This brand of styrene offers a huge range of different sections, sheets and strip. Imported from the USA, Evergreen has gained in popularity with Modern Image modellers, especially for industrial structures and wagon scratchbuilding. An excellent booklet is available which details all material sections and basic techniques for cutting and working.

Slaters Plasticard
A standard material, readily available from virtually all model shops. Slaters supply styrene card in black and standard opaque white. The patterned range is embossed rather than machined, losing some definition as a result.

Fineline Styrene
Scratchbuilders will find this range of considerable value, due to the huge selection of moulded styrene sections, pipes, rods, ladders and half round sections.

Fillers
As a stock item in the workshop, model fillers find many uses in all modelling applications (as well as some domestic situations - but avoid letting the management know). Many modellers prefer the car body shop type fillers, but I have tended to favour 'Milliput'. This is the trade name for a small range of two part epoxy type fillers. The standard type is the yellow/grey filler, most commonly used by modellers. A second is white Milliput, with a finer texture and finds use in detailed artistic applications and repairs. Hardened Milliput of either type is eas-ily cut, sanded to a good finish, drilled, tapped, turned and filed. To use Milliput, cut off equal parts of the two rolls of filler included in each pack. Knead these for a few moments to soften them before blending the two parts together. This blending, usually done by hand, mixes the two parts so they will set. Kneading should continue until the filler is an even colour. Now it is ready to use as a flexible putty which may be applied to the model with an old scalpel blade. A touch of water will assist with smoothing the filler surface.

Adhesives
What would we do without the sticky stuff? From the water soluble PVA glues used universally for ballasting of track formations to the highly sophisticated cyanoacrylate adhesives, there's a glue for all modelling applications.

WARNING. All adhesives are hazardous to health, so handle them with care. Store in secure cupboards to prevent children finding them. Be prepared to wear safety glasses and gloves, especially when handling the very liquid superglues. Protect your surroundings from accidental spillage. Ventilate the working area adequately. Splashes to the skin must be removed immediately, seek medical advice if irritation occurs.

A complete model of a Dace ballast wagon constructed from an AME kit. The axleguards and solebars are cast as one assembly, so compensation is best installed using the MJT internal unit.

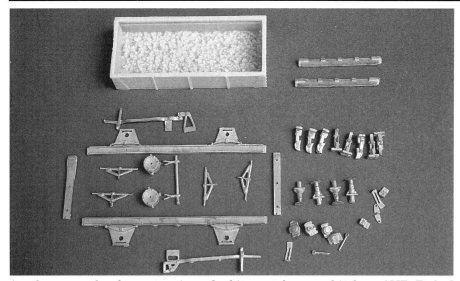

Another example of a cast resin and white metal wagon kit from AME. Etched brass seems to have fallen out of favour in this format.

Splashes to the eye must be irrigated with clean water. Seek immediate medical attention.

Cyanoacrylate Adhesives (Superglues)

Superglue has solved many of the problems associated with bonding different materials, and is available in various forms, from the very watery to gels. The time you have for positioning the parts is limited although gel types allow more than the standard glues. Most superglues cannot perform if surfaces are not clean or keyed by roughening with a file. Successful bonding depends on the contact area of parts being glued; any gaps will weaken that bond, which explains why some small parts do not bond successfully.

Useful cyanoacrylates recently introduced are the 'Zap a Gap' range, available in several forms suitable for the modeller. Performance is enhanced by the accelerating agent - this 'Zip Kicker' crystallises the adhesive instantly, a great help when difficult assembly jobs require instant bonds. The best way to apply any superglue is to place a spot onto a piece of scrap plasticard and use a blunt scalpel blade to transfer the glue. Never apply the glue direct to the model from the bottle.

Solvent Adhesives

Solvent adhesives work by the localised melting of styrene. They give a clean, neat finish not normally associated with polystyrene cement. Apply with a small paint brush, typically a No.1 or No.0 size brush, ensuring that only sparing amounts reach the model. Plastic softened by the solvent swiftly hardens again, but will take finger prints and other marks in the meantime, so handle with care. Slaters' Mek Pak is popular amongst modellers today for all plastic wagon kit construction. It is mild in its action but of course, toxic, so handle with care. There are alternatives to Mek Pak, including Humbrol Liquid

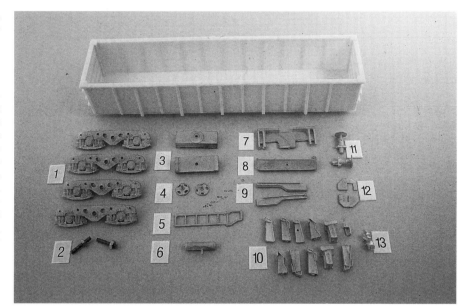

Bogie wagons are considerably simplified with bogies cast in white metal and the bodies cast in resin. This leaves small detailing components to add, with superglue or Araldite. Parts shown are: 1 Axle Motion Bogies; 2 Studding for bogie pivot; 3 Bogie spacers; 4 Brake wheels; 5 Ladder; 6 Air tank; 7 'Outer' headstocks; 8 'Inner' headstocks; 9 Outer Bracing; 10 Underframe bracing; 11 Oleo buffers (two only on an outer wagon); 12 Rotary coupling housing; 13 Airbrake Distributor.

Poly, 'Daywat Poly' and 'Plastic Weld', a very powerful solvent regarded as too strong for plastic kit construction and styrene card. ABS type plastics require the strength of 'Plastic Weld' to bond, but not styrene of less than 100thou, so keep 'Plastic Weld' for special applications.

Epoxy

The brands most commonly used by modellers is Araldite 'Rapid' and Devcon, both of which save time over the standard stuff. That said, the big disadvantage of epoxy resin glues remains the curing time. Even the 'five minute' type will require more than this to cure and achieve full strength. Epoxy gives you the time to adjust parts into position before the glue sets; it acts as a filler when required and copes with poorly prepares surfaces, advantages not normally found with superglues.

Epoxy resin glues are prepared for use by mixing equal amounts of adhesive and hardening compound, sometimes a wasteful process because one normally

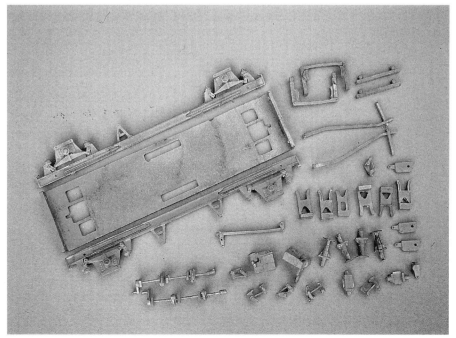

AME Underframe kit for the Hornby MGR model.

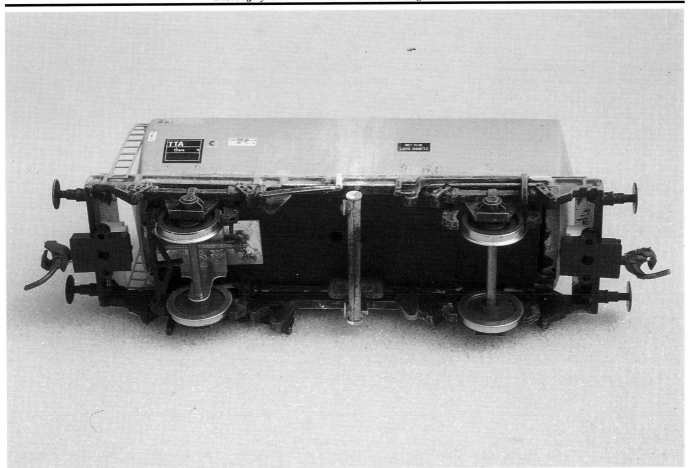

Above and below. **Underframe kits are available from several manufacturers. AME dominates the modern prototype scene, including in its range the universally useful TTA underframe, found under many different prototypes.**

has to mix more than required for the job in hand.

Tools

The large selection of ex-surgical tools available from the trade are ideal for wagon modelling. Use quality modelling tools, and remember that poor tools will contribute to poor results. Most wagon building projects only involve simple implements: scalpels, rulers, squares and files.

Cutting; Knives and Scalpels

Blades for the Swan Morton surgical scalpel handles come in all shapes for paring plastic detail. Straight blades are good for scoring styrene sheet, for snap cutting. One big mistake made by many modellers is overuse of blades before changing them. Dull scalpel blades are, quite frankly, dangerous to both yourself and the model; blunt blades will slip and skid on plastic surfaces.

Always work with the blade pointing away from you and do not take unnecessary risks with new blades. Scalpel blades may be changed by gripping the old blade with a pair of pliers for removal from the handle. Always fit the new one with pliers, too. Wrapping the blade in a small piece of masking tape is additional insurance against injury. Once removed, the old blade has useful functions for transferring tiny amounts of cyanoacrylate adhesive to the modelling work. Dispose of used blades responsibly by wrapping them in masking tape and placing in old film containers.

Exacto produce fine cutting tools as separate items or in complete box sets of craft knife blades and handles. At the very least, invest in an Exacto razor saw which will prove its worth in cutting the larger plastic parts. The ubiquitous 'Stanley Knife' is a must for all modellers, notwithstanding its value in big modelling projects. This is the nuclear part of your tool arsenal, complementing your finer scalpels and craft knives.

Cutting; other tools

The side cutters and Xuron shears are the correct tools for handrail wire and fine metal sections. The Xuron shears are by far the best for clean accurate cutting of thicker material sections. I have come to rely on good quality hairdressers' scissors for removing small etched details from frets.

Cutting Mats

Come in a variety of sizes and may be obtained from any craft shop. Sizes range from A1 (expensive) to A5, usually coloured green and with a printed grid and scale. They are useful for protecting work surfaces and preventing the premature blunting of scalpel blades. Cutting mats

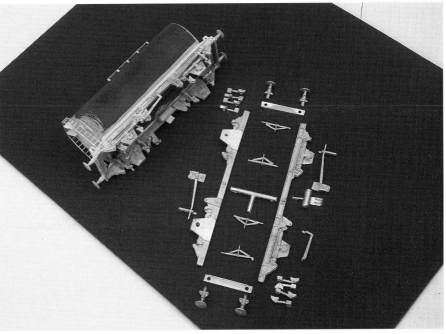

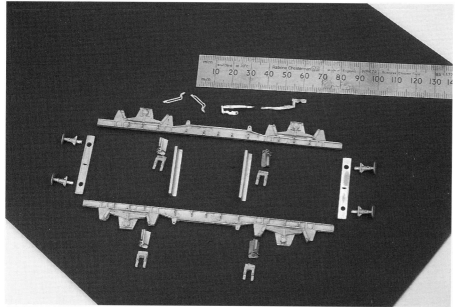

AME underframe for the Hornby VDA airbraked van. In the case of the Hornby MGR and VDA models, purchasing the body as a spare keeps the cost down.

are remarkable as they heal well after quite major cuts and slashes. Protect them from spillages of glue, paint and solvents in order to get the best performance.

Pin Vice and Twist drills
By far the most useful device is a pinvice or pinchuck, a form of small hand drill usually with knurled handles and collets at one or both ends. They can hold drills from 3mm to 0.3mm in diameter, depending on the type you have. The slow action of these hand drills gives a high order of control, avoiding the risk of melting plastic through friction. Twist drill bits are essential for detailing and rebuilding RTR models. I have invested in a full set supplied in a carrying box with a sliding lid. This offered me drill sizes of 0.3mm to 1.5mm in useful 0.1mm increments, with each drill bit carefully identified and safely transported in its own slot. If you are starting out, add a 0.5mm, 0.8mm, 1.0mm, 1.5 and 2.0mm twist drills to your shopping list.

Fibreglass Pencil and Sticks
Ideal tools for cleaning and burnishing components made from etched brass and white metal. They have an abrasive cleaning action which removes excess adhesive and solder. The fibreglass pencil is a propelling type with fine heads of fibres used for cleaning fine work. Fibreglass sticks are better for cleaning large work pieces.

The glass fibres wear off and can prove irritating ESPECIALLY to the eyes, though some people seem more affected than others. Be safe and step outside to use them.

Files
One essential is a wallet or two of reasonable quality needle files. Keep a couple of large fine and medium cut files for heavy duty work. I keep two sets, a good one for filing tabs from etchings and for moulded plastics and a second, less salubrious, set reserved for white metal, fillers, soft plastic and solder - all these clog files like mad. Quite a variety of shapes

are found in a file wallet, the square and flat files being the most useful for our purposes. To care for files, use a suede brush to clear the muck and swarf clogging the cutting surface.

Pliers
Fine nosed pliers come in handy for all sorts of jobs; bending handrail wire, gripping scalpel blades, folding brass etchings and as a general method of holding things for filing and cutting.

Steel Rules and Squares
Very much a functional tool, arm yourself with a 300mm and a 150mm steel rule. Use the longer one for measuring and cutting of materials, reserving the smaller rule for measuring only. Keep rules for joinery away from those for modelling and purchase the very best you can afford. Small engineers' squares are absolutely worth every penny. Also keep a couple of plastic drawing squares at hand to check larger pieces of work, remembering that the edges are not suitable for cutting.

Tweezers
Tweezers made from metal with fine ends are the best for our purposes and offer considerable versatility in all modelling techniques. Keep and use the plastic cover supplied with the tweezers so the fine ends do not become bent or twisted in the tool box.

Broaches
Similar in appearance to some shaped files, broaches are cutting tools for opening undersized holes. Cutting edges along their length pare material away from the edges; the resulting work will be neater and undertaken with greater control than with a file.

Soldering Kit
A 25 watt iron will cope with most soldering jobs, but if you are considering soldering of white metal components you need a suitable soldering iron controller for reducing the iron tip temperature. Choose the correct solders and fluxes for each job.

Styrene Cutting Tools
Scratch builders working with styrene strip will find theAcme Tool Co. 'chopper' useful for repetitive cutting jobs. This company also produces a small range of devices for styrene embossing, cutting and preparation. They save time and effort, but are not essential to wagon kit building.

A simple device to make yourself is a styrene sheet cutting board. Two 300mm rulers set at 90 degrees to each other fixed to an offcut of kitchen worktop is perfect for squaring up new sheets, accurate cutting and swift production of duplicate pieces.

White Metal Soldering
The key to success with white metal wagon and bogie kits
White metal causes more grief than all the other modelling materials. While steam era modellers find white metal kit

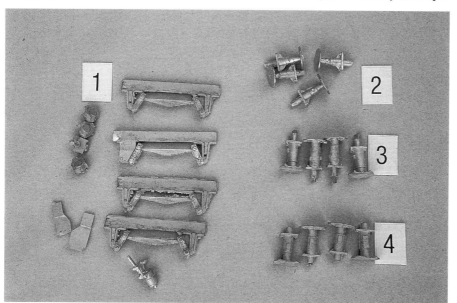

AME Underframe conversion for the Parkside Dundas vanwide model. The parts are for the airbraked MOD VEA version.

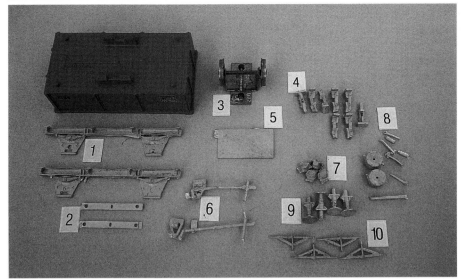

Simple underframe for the Hornby MSV Barbel stone tippler wagon body: 1 Solebar axleguard castings; 2 Headstocks; 3 MJT internal compensation unit; 4 Clasp brake shoes; 5 Floor plate; 6 Brake levers; 7 SKF axleboxes; 8 Vacuum cylinder assemblies; 9 Buffers; 10 Brake trusses.

construction run of the mill (the skills are learned as a matter of course when building loco kits) others, such as modern image modellers, rarely need to solder brass or white metal. Beginners to the hobby, without the benefit of the relevant techniques, find themselves at a disadvantage with simple white metal kits such as bogies.

Glue is not an ideal solution to the white metal kit problem, for it often re-

Compensation Units. This is the internal type, suitable for ready to run models and those kits which include the solebars and axleguards as one casting. 10BA studding and nuts ensure a reliable rocking unit - studding and nuts are not supplied by MJT however.

sults in a weaker assembly, prone to damage or loss of detail. Once you try white metal soldering techniques, you will realise that it is a matter of confidence, your skill level graduating to composite metal soldering - white metal to brass, white metal to aluminium and so on.

Modellers fight shy of white metal soldering for many reasons - they prefer superglues (believing they bond like, well, super glue!), they fear melting critical components, or they lack correct tools and equipment. Many are more at home with

etched brass and plasticard (no melt down risk here!).

Any of the above sound familiar? There are other factors too, but the end result is the same, dissatisfaction with the finished result. The model which pushed me over the brink was the Appleby Model Engineering (AME) carbon dioxide tank wagon kit. I wanted it and used it to nail the soldering jinx once and for all. Two of the kits were duly purchased and advice sought from other modellers who had built some of the most complicated white metal kits available. (What? You can't solder white metal? What are you modern modellers coming to?)

I started with my trusty Antex soldering iron; at 25 Watts its high tip temperature is quite capable of melting cast components with ease. An SRB soldering iron controller fitted to the mains lead reduces the tip temperature. For greater flexibility, fit the controller to a short length of extension lead so any iron may

be used. The controller itself has a control knob, to vary the heat in line with the application. The scale is a simple one - half position on the controller will reduce the tip heat by half.

The technique involves the adjustment of the soldering iron to a temperature which melts the low melt solder but not the cast components alongside. Finding the small temperature window between the melting points of the solder and white metal is the key to success. Careful work adjusting the controller knob and application of the soldering iron to an unimportant part of the kit will calibrate it. Be aware that all kits are not cast from the same metal, so this calibration exercise is required for every project.

The actual mechanics of soldering white metal is little different to brass from this point onwards. Clean the parts to be joined with a fibreglass pencil, apply the flux to the correct areas using an old paint brush then simply apply heat and a small amount of solder. The flux sizzles, the solder melts and flows to make a good joint. Once cool, the joint should be strong and stable. Any movements during the cooling of the solder will weaken or destroy the bond, making a further application of heat necessary. Generally higher temperatures are required to desolder a bond because of the alloying effect of solder with the white metal parts. Take great care because higher temperatures may melt the parts being soldered.

White metal components do not get as hot during soldering. Larger pieces may be held in your fingers whilst applying heat, so the use of Carrs' hot tape, clamps or pegs is avoided.

The SRB soldering iron controller has other uses too. Adjust the temperature to melt 145 degree detailing solder for brass kits whilst leaving undisturbed 188 degree or higher temperature solders used in the main construction. The old adage 'never glue if you can solder' is still very valid.

Cambrian Models Bogie Kits
Cambrian were the first to break the modern wagon log jam by producing bogie kits for their plastic products and releasing them as separate items. First was the Gloucester bogie for the Lima Seacow ballast hopper wagon. They followed this with a FBT6 and Y25C types for various steel wagon kits. They all suffered from flimsy design and poor performance. The simple answer is to modify them with A1-Railmatch etched brass spacers, giving greater strength and better performance. They lack the advantage of white metal construction which offers useful mass and durability.

Mendip Models Bogie Kits
Cast in white metal, this small range of bogie kits covers the common types such as FTB6 and Y25C. They are beautifully engineered with spacers which simply clip into recesses in the rear of the bogie sideframes. These may be glued or soldered into place. Cosmetic detail includes suspension spring details cast right to the rear of the frames. End spacers are sup-

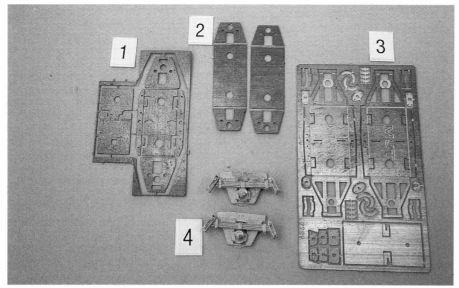

Axleguard etches, both compensated and uncompensated types. 1.BR Tracking Duty 2. Low floor container wagon axleguards (A1 Railmatch) 3. Classic 'W' irons 4. Mendip Models Heavy Duty with Bruningham Springs.

plied with the FBT6, Y25C and VNH1 bogie types. The bogie spacer is common to all Mendip Models bogie kits, cast with a central pivot hole and a slot to accept a coupling bar (supplied). When assembling them, be sure to fit the spacer slot upwards. Coupling bars themselves are adapted to accept a Hornby or Bachmann type tension lock coupling. Coupling bars may be cut to the required length with a scalpel, to obtain the correct coupling distance between wagons.

top hat (Maygib or Romford) bearings before placing to one side.

The central spacers will need several holes drilling to achieve a good fit. Commence by drilling a 2.2mm diameter hole through the spacers to act as a pivot hole. This needs modification by angling the drill when forming the hole so the pivot is not too rigid. Follow up by drilling the side holes to a depth of 5mm using a 1.5mm drill. These aid the assembly of the sideframes to the spacers. Sol-

tion of trying to hold three pieces of plastic (sideframes and spacer) together while plastic softened by solvent hardens sufficiently to clip in wheels and bearings. You need to keep it all square and somehow stop the four cup bearings from dropping out and falling to the floor with the wheels.

All may be in place, after expletives and sometimes stuck fingers, and we can fit our bogies to the wagon and test run it. However, things are not quite right, a bogie may be out of true because the plastic on the spacer melted just a little too much. There is nothing more frustrating than to discover a three legged bogie, the fourth wheel refusing to make contact with the rail. Even worse! The plastic is brittle and will not flex slightly to permit adjustments. SNAP! Back to square one.

Nonetheless, all bogie kits are invaluable to the modern modeller, offering excellent and accurate detail, though they are sometimes let down by indifferent technical design of the support bits. It is important to note that not all bogie kits suffer from this malaise, and indeed some kit manufacturers have done an excellent job. I use a lot of bogie kits from many manufacturers but reliability is of the utmost importance. I know other modellers need reliability of operation too.

So, what are we to do? Easy. We replace the supporting bits like spacers with something more robust. What is needed is a new spacer unit to which the cosmetic sideframes with their fine detail may be assembled. A1-Railmatch produce such an item and believe me, what a relief it is to banish the bogie problems completely.

To use, simply snip the frame from the fret and remove any etched tabs with a fine cut file. Start by folding the spacer strips at 90 degrees, with fold lines on the inside. Then fold the sideframes into place, locating them with a small fillet of solder. There is more than one axle hole position provided, and it is left to you to choose the correct wheelbase. Offer your cosmetic sideframe up to the etch and mark the most suitable holes. Open up the holes slightly with a broach and fit Maygib top hat bearings.

Open out the axle holes in the rear of the cosmetic sideframes, being careful not to drill right through the axlebox detail. These are soldered to the etched frame for strength. Plastic sideframes from Cambrian are applied with superglue. Clip in the wheels and adjust to ensure that the bogie sits square on an offcut of plate glass. There we have it, a P4, EM and OO compatible etched bogie frame for those frustrating plastic and cast whitemetal bogie jobs.

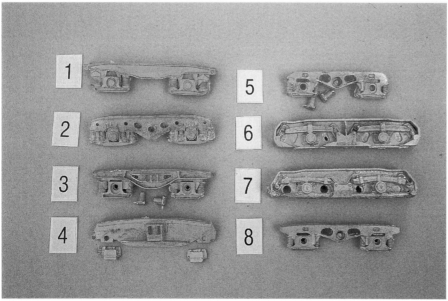

Bogie sideframes: 1 GPS25; 2 BSC Axle Motion; 3 Fabricated Y25C; 4 8' Plateback; 5 Y27C; 6 German DB665; 7 German coil wagon bogie; 8 Cast Y25 *aka* VNH1.

AME Bogie Kits

You may wish to assemble the bogies as per the instructions supplied with the kit. Whilst the cosmetic detail is beautifully executed, all axle holes and pivot holes must be drilled out from solid metal, which is harder than you may think. Some modellers encounter problems with this aspect whilst finding the rest of AME kits ridiculously simple.

Remove all casting flash and follow up with a fibre pencil. Fit a 2mm twist drill to a pinvice and drill out the axle boxes carefully from the rear. Fit 2mm

der with low melt solder and a temperature controlled iron. Such is the rigidity of this assembly, that the running wheels are effectively held permanently, so take care not to damage them with heat or solder flux.

Bogie Problems Solved

The moulded plastic bogies supplied in some wagon kits are problematic by being fiddly to assemble, brittle when complete and unreliable in operation. I think that we have all experienced the frustra-

Underframe Kits

Tucked away in the extensive catalogues of 4mm scale wagon kits and component manufacturers are useful underframe kits and components intended to replace ready to run mouldings and assist scratchbuilders. By far the most useful underframe kits for modern prototypes are produced by Cambrian, Mendip Models, Parkside Dundas and AME. Those produced by Cambrian and Parkside are moulded in plastic, usually for vacuum braked BR standard wagons. They produce detailing parts for underframe work, suspension units, brake wheels and plastic axleguards. AME underframe kits are more sophisticated, requiring careful assembly to obtain the best from them. From the modern modellers point of view, underframe kits from Mendip Models and AME are the most important.

AME kit no 4U04 TTA tank wagon underframe

Use the AME TTA underframe kit as superdetailed replacement for the Hornby plastic one. Examination of photographs of aggregate and scrap steel wagons will demonstrate the universality of this kit, for a variety of prototypes. The TTA type underframe appears under various LPG and bitumen tanks; china clay wagons and departmental vehicles too. It's an excellent starting point for many satisfying scratchbuilding projects and makes a good introduction to white metal underframe kits and soldering techniques.

This particular kit represents the modernised version with Bruninghaus springs and airbrakes. It's not suitable for modelling earlier versions of the 45t tank wagon, say pre-1978. For modernised fleets of Shell, BP and Esso tanks, for example, this underframe kit is ideal.

When modelling other vehicles, such as the Tigerail POA wagons, be sure that the prototype measurements represented by the kit fit your chosen subject. You need to choose wagons with a 4,572mm (15ft) wheelbase and 7,824mm (25ft 8in) length over headstocks. Allow for airbrakes, 8 shoe clasp friction brakes and standard wagon Oleo buffers.

To make a good job of assembling any of the underframe kits from AME, you will need the following materials and tools.

- 2mm diameter top hat bearings
- 12mm diameter disc wheels
- 20 thou styrene card. MJT internal compensation unit (optional)
- Fibre glass pencil
- Selection of files
- 2mm twist drill
- Pin vice, sheet of glass
- 70 degree low melt solder and flux
- Temperature controlled soldering iron
- Basic modelling tools listed in this chapter

The AME TTA underframe kit is comprehensive indeed; you will find 26 castings, everything from solebar and axleguard assemblies to clasp brake shoes, tank discharge pipes and buffers. Some casting flash is inevitable so this must be removed from components before assembling the underframe. Use a 2mm twist drill to open out the axleboxes. Make the mistake of leaving this small job until the underframe is complete and drilling out those axleboxes will prove to be awkward indeed.

Solder together the headstocks/ solebars sub-assembly. Clip in a set of workshop wheels to check that all is square and running true. A soldered underframe may be gently teased into shape without the worry of breaking any

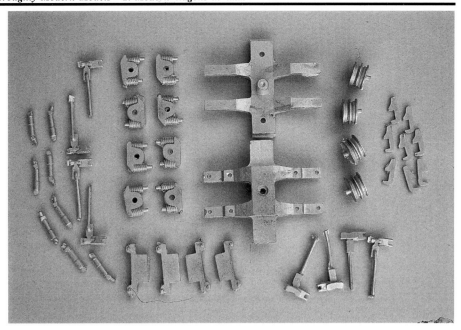

ARC Powell Duffryn low trackforce bogie kit. (AME).

bonds. Add the brake block assemblies to the rear of the solebars; the wheels now help you to align the brake shoes correctly. Brake rigging can be added to the backs of the blocks with the apex facing towards the axle. All that is left is the air reservoir tank, brake levers, the SAB adjuster and buffers. Enhance the underframe with A1-Railmatch turned brass buffers, MJT coupling hooks and Roco airbrake pipes.

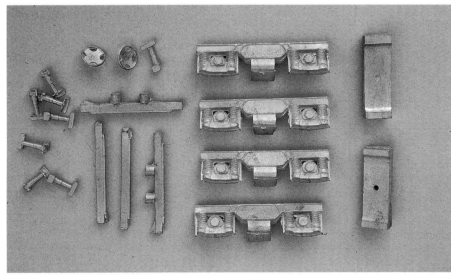

Shlieren Bogie for tank wagons.

Compensation may be achieved using MJT internal rocking units. A Hornby TTA tank barrel has a reasonably flat base, ideal for fixing a compensation rocking unit from MJT. A false floor is essential to accommodate the rocking unit if any other wagon type is being modelled. Remember to keep the axle holes in the axleguards at the other end for the fixed axle or you will have some fun getting the wagon to run.

AME kit No 4U05 for VAA, VBA and VCA. (Also Hornby OAA and PFA container flat wagon)

The central part of this underframe is the inner frame casting, which I found to be

slightly too narrow when dry assembled and checked against some wheel sets. This is not a serious problem, but requires a slightly different approach to that outlined in the kit instructions. On a flat or plane surface using a quality engineers' square, the solebar and headstock castings are soldered together to form the basic underframe. Clip in workshop wheels to make any adjustments (not usually necessary if you have drilled accurate axle holes and used the flat surface for assembly). The inner frame is added at this point - fillets of solder fill the gap between solebars and frame. File back to give a neat appearance to the model.

The instructions caution us as to the differences in each solebar and the Vee hangers. One has a solid hanger, for the short brake lever. The other side has an open Vee hanger which accepts the long brake lever. Behind the open Vee hanger, solder the airtank into position.

The tiny cast details supplied require vigilance to locate them in the right places. Identify and fit the two SAB levers which fit behind the solebars and

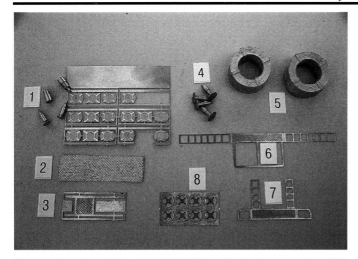

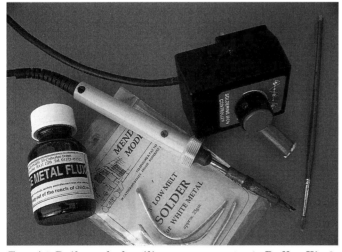

Top. A1 Railmatch detailing components. 1. Buffer Kit 2. Checkerplate 3. Ballast wagon guard's 4. Freight Oleo buffers 5. Skel coil loads 6/7. Etched walkways for Hornby and Lima PGA wagons 8. Brake wheels.
Middle. MJT detailing components. 1. Coupling hooks - cosmetic 2. Heavy duty buffers 3. Dowty buffer 4. Leaf springs for BR vac. braked standard wagon 5. Brake disc insets for wheels 6. Oil axleboxes 7. Vacuum pipes 8. Oval buffers.
Bottom. Bare essentials for soldering white metal kits.

Buffers and an MJT cast coupling hook completes the underframe; a working instanter coupling may be installed with ease if required.

AME Kit No 4U02 for Hornby VDA vans. (Also OTA timber wagons, ZCA 'Sea Urchin' and runner wagons)

This kit differs slightly from kit 4U05. Return to your flat surface and square for the solebar and inner spacer assembly; the inner spacers fit to the inner face of the lugs cast into the rear of the solebars, flush with the solebar tops. Clip in the works wheelsets to check that all is square and true. The headstocks are next, the ends of the solebars locating into the recesses. Check once again to see if everything is square, adjusting as necessary. There are few small parts for this underframe; commence by assembling disc brake callipers and fitting these to the rear of the solebars aligned with the wheels.

Complete assembly with the finely cast brake levers (two very short ones this time) secured to the right side of one solebar in the case of the cranked type and opposite in the case of the straight one.

the dismantling of one wheel set, filing off the axle points and then reassembling the wheel set to the compensation unit. The inner bearings are etched with holes to accept the standard 2mm diameter axle and spacing washers are supplied if required.

A tiny spot of cyanoacrylate adhesive is all that is required to fix the compensation assembly to the floor of the model, but do be sure that the axle is square to the solebars and the unit is centrally positioned. The opposite axle is left fixed, running in 2mm bearings fixed to the cosmetic axleguard and with no sideplay whatsoever. This ensures that the wagon rides level while the compensation enables the model to ride safely over the bumps.

Installing Compensation W Irons (Axleguards)

A wide variety of etched brass compensation W irons (also referred to as axleguards) are available from MJT, A1-Railmatch and D&S Models, to mention but a few. They are designed for two axle, fixed wheelbase wagons, for cosmetic detailing and for the fitting of 2mm diameter bearings. Generally, modern image modellers will find the BR heavy duty axleguards available from MJT, A1-Railmatch and the various finescale society stores the most useful. Any type of compensation W iron may serve if they are used as a basic frame for cast white metal axleguard suspension units from Mendip Models or AME. Castings are large enough to conceal the brass frame, which may be incorrect for many modern wagon types. Mendip produce a Bruninghaus fitted heavy duty axleguard and AME offer Gloucester MK2 and BSC suspension units. Using W irons helps to get axleguard detail square and true, a critical feature for good running qualities.

Vacuum braked BR Standard wagons may be modelled using the superb range of cast axle box, spring and brake detail from MJT. This detail is designed to fit etched brass W irons either rigged for compensation or fitted 'solid' to the wagon floor. The AME VEA/ODA underframe conversion kit also benefits from BR standard W irons, rather than the plastic mouldings on the Parkside vanwide and tube wagon kits. Assembly of most manufacturers' W iron kits is straightforward. Fold the etches with fold lines on the inside. Fix with a tiny fillet of solder. Two assemblies are required per wagon, a 'solid' one fixed to a piece of 40thou styrene and the other clipped to spigots on a baseplate supplied with the W irons. Units rock from side to side on the spigots as long as the baseplate is fitted to the wagon carefully, with sparing amounts of adhesive.

An alternative method for assembling a rocking W iron is to use 10BA studding as a rocking axis. Solder a length to the W iron with spare on either side, to which 10BA nuts are fitted. Then solder the nuts to a brass baseplate so the assembly rocks smoothly. Care is needed with your soldering, don't lock it up solid. When assembling the W iron baseplate

make contact with the bottom of the suspension hangers. Locate and install the brake push rods, the short one to the left and the long one to the right. There is a gap between the two which will accept the brake pivot lever. To this is fitted the SAB unit itself which locates on the inner frame.

Any soldering operation must be precise and swift. Linger with even a temperature controlled iron and you may lose your brake push rods to excessive heat.

Installing Internal Compensation Units

The best method of installing compensation to ready to run underframes and kits is by using an inside bearing rocking unit. MJT inside bearing rocking units are intended for models where the cosmetic suspension and axle guard detail is fixed to the solebars. Any modeller familiar with normal compensation axleguard sets will find the inner compensation units simple to assemble, the only difference being

A1 Railmatch produce two etched bogie frames, shown on the left is the 8'6" sprinter bogie frame equipped with sprinter type bogies. Builders of Mk3 based EMU stock (post 1983) may be interested to note that the etch has extensions for a shoe beam. The bogie in the centre and to the right is the freight bogie frame made up with two types of cosmetic sideframes: a Gloucester bogie, seen fitted to the Sheerness Steel bogie scrap wagon and a plastic Y25C from Cambrian. The etched frame adds a lot of strength and stability to cosmetic sideframes by replacing the cast metal of plastic spacers provided in the original bogie kits.

sub-assembly to the floor, make careful measurements to ensure they are square to the solebars and are free of glue and solder. Then fit the cosmetic suspension and axlebox detail.

Buffers

Wagon buffers have featured in the A1-Railmatch, MJT and AME ranges for many years now. Both MJT and AME produce excellent buffers cast in white metal. MJT concentrate on older prototypes and buffers for BR Standard wagons. AME covers the era of airbraked vehicles with useful samples of buffers for continental ferry vans and other vehicles. Of the eleven buffer types offered in past issues of the

A1-Railmatch catalogue (all turned in brass), only three were suitable for wagons. The method of fixing is simple; drill a suitable hole to provide a tight fit and fix with cyanoacrylate adhesive. A1-Railmatch has recently added new designs of buffers to their catalogue of modern detailing parts, to take account of the new types used on British locomotives and continental registered wagons. Packs A30 and A31 both show a change in format from the traditional turned brass shank and buffer head to one of a separate etched head and turned brass shank. The cost of preparing bras rod extrusions to the various new profiles has proved to be prohibitive, so the buffer heads are etched in stainless steel to the correct profiles. The etching process has permitted the addition of detail onto the reverse side of the buffer head, a feature not possible to replicate in brass turning. The shanks

themselves are turned in brass and are a universal unit in each pack; they may be glued to the buffer heads with cyanoacrylate type adhesive.

The buffer packs are straightforward to use and should cause few problems. Commence by removing the chosen etched buffer heads from the fret with a good pair of tin snips or cutters. Although the etched tabs are quite thin, stainless steel is an unforgiving material, guaranteed to dull the cutting edge of scissors. The buffer heads may be profiled to recreate the shape of the prototype by careful bending in the fingers. Fix the universal shank to the buffer heads with a thick

type cyanoacrylate adhesive, which should be left to set for a decent interval before fitting to the model in the same manner as traditional buffer sets.

Pack A31 comes with a different type of shank from that supplied in pack A30. The shank is an inverted stepped one, commonly found on freight stock. Careful observation of the prototype is required to ensure that the correct buffer head is used. The new format is a departure from the previously accepted method of adding buffers to our ready to run models, but has been designed to keep the cost within acceptable limits.

The value of such brass frames is very important to wagon scratch builders by providing a secure base for cosmetic sideframes. The brace of Polybulks are equipped with Cambrian Y25C plastic sideframes fitted to the A1 Railmatch etched frames. Strength and reliability of running are the main objectives of these items, especially important for exhibition use. The frames accept standard Romford 2mm top hat bearings, with 8BA studding, cheese head screws and nuts ideal for the installation of bogies to the wagon.

Many of the former VDA vans find employment as REA barrier wagons for movement of LUL stock. One end, REA No.210282 is fitted with a special adapter coupling. Didcot June 1997.

Experimental suspension fitted VDA No.201025 provides brake force for LUL stock movements. This wagon is finished in EWS livery, transfers for which may be obtained from AME. Didcot June 1997.

CHAPTER THREE
Railfreight Van Projects

Simple but satisfying modelling projects sometimes start from a collection of ready to run models purchased second-hand or from readily available plastic kits. The Hornby VDA van and the Parkside vanwide kit are good examples. They are simple to detail or convert to different types, and are appropriate for many layouts. Other models suitable for detailing and conversion include Fertiliser vans (Lima) and VGA sliding wall door vans, originally produced as a kit and now as a ready to run release by Bachmann.

Making the best of the Hornby Railfreight Van

Hornby have produced a basic model for the once standard 20ft. 9in. wheelbase AB van for many years now, supplemented from time to time with relatively inaccurate but useful models of the Procor and Campbell's Soup curtain sided vans (TOPS code PVA). The 'standard' Hornby van (TOPS code VDA) makes use of a universal underframe derived from their OAA and SAA models, an understandable compromise to keep development costs to a minimum. I suspect that the

van body is a little on the narrow side, but only in the region of 2mm, not enough to spoil it for many modellers.

Since I first discussed the merits or otherwise of these models in *Railway Modeller* (January 1988) there are new developments from the trade to consider, such as conversion parts and underframe kits. The AB vans from the Speedlink era are classic vehicles which merit a place on all layouts dated from the start of the 1970s. They still operate today in departmental, Ministry of Defence and revenue use. Many redundant vans were rebuilt into one of a variety of types, such as timber or runner vehicles, rebuilds which make good modelling subjects in their own right, using ready to run products as a basis.

Conversion of the Hornby curtain sided van to earlier variants of Railfreight AB vans is a simple conversion project, with little need for complicated detailing. Etched brass overlays are available from A1-Models for the VAA, VBA and VCA vans. Enhancement of the Hornby VDA van is easier still; simply remove the roof ventilator and repaint in your chosen livery. There is enough prototype material to keep you going for many hours of satisfying modelling with this group of wagons alone!

Help from the Trade

The excellent brass overlays from A1-Models (A1-Railmatch) have been available for many years. They also produce other detailing parts, including 18in. freight Oleo buffers turned in brass, air tanks, brake disc inserts and bufferbeam detail.

Valuable support comes from Appleby Model Engineering (AME) in the form of excellent underframe kits for the VAA, VBA, VCA, and VDA wagons, supplied as white metal castings and a vast range of smaller detailing components, too many to list here. (Go on, buy a catalogue!).

Paint and transfers come from Railmatch, Phoenix Paints, Fox Transfers, Replica Railways and 'Lineside Look'. Make sure you include the HAZCHEM diamonds commonly seen on vans conveying materials between the various MOD sites.

Modelling work for the VAA/VBA, VCA and VDA vans

Take care to select the correct pack of etched brass van sides from A1-Railmatch. Dismantle the model, putting the underframe to one side for treatment later unless you intend to replace it with something a little more realistic. The buffers on the underframe double as body retaining clips and, likely enough, at least one will break in the process. Although they may be refitted, the problem is solved permanently by opting for turned brass replacements.

RAILFREIGHT AB VANS: VARIANTS AND REBUILDS

Number Sequence	Build date	Lot No	Type/TOPS
200000-200208	1969-70	3685	VAA VBA
			ZDA Departmental
			ZRA Departmental
			RBA Runner wagon
200209	1972	3739	VBA
200210-200219E	1970	3725	VBA
200220-200228E	1970	3686	VBA
200230-200238E	1970	3687	VBA
200240-200249E	1969	3696	VBA
200250-200324	1970-1	3726	VBA
			ZCA Sea Urchin
200325-200448	1971-2	3764	VCA
			FPA container flats
			ZEA Departmental
			ZRA Departmental
200450-200549	1974	3832	VCA
			FPA Container flats
			ZEA Departmental
			ZRA Departmental
200550-200649	1974-5	3840	VBA
			ZCA Sea Urchin
200650-200997	1976	3855	VDA
			OTA Timber wagon
			RRA/RLA Operational
			ZCA Sea Urchin open
			ZDA Departmental
201000-201099E	1975-6	3856	VDA
			OTA Timber wagon
			ZDA/ZRA/ZXA Departmental
210100-210399	1977-8	3908	VDA
			OTA Timber Wagon
			ZCA Sea Urchin open
			ZDA Departmental
			REA/RLA/ZEA/ZRA

Note that E = Experimental Suspensions

Top. **Close up of the suspension unit, TOPS panel and door opening equipment of experimental suspension fitted VDA 201025. Didcot June 1997.**

Middle. **Close up of adapter coupling on REA barrier wagon. The standard suspension fitted to VDA vans is shown.**

Bottom. **VDA No.T210195 is painted in a non-standard promotional livery, to advertise the successful Transrail Enterprise network. This will be an historical curiosity in a few years' time. The body colour is flint grey with a vast 'Big T' logo. Didcot, August 1997.**

Remove all 'proud' detail such as strapping tags, end ribs and rippled curtain effect from the body. A No.23 blade mounted into a Swan Morton No.4 handle is an ideal tool, but remember to replace the blades frequently as they become dulled with use. Some work is required at the van ends, smoothing down the plastic to achieve the flush effect common on this series of vans. Hornby moulded a strange ventilator to the roof of all its AB vans. Care must be exercised when removing this, to keep the nice curved profile of the roof. The moulding is partly pared down without gouging the plastic, and the rest removed with a file and smoothed off with 800 grit wet and dry paper. A roof rib is lost as a result, so replace it with thin styrene strip. (10thou by 10thou).

Offer up your chosen brass sides and mark in the position of the door openers. These are located to the lower edge of the van side. (Use reference photographs!). Drill out the plastic to leave a space behind the door opening which may be backed with 40thou styrene card. Glue pieces of 20thou styrene card into the openings, to reduce the depth.

Once satisfied with the fit of the sides, mix Araldite 'Rapid' or Devcon two part epoxy glue and apply it swiftly to the prepared bodysides. Fit the replacement sides using clothes pegs to hold everything in place until the glue has set (in approximately five minutes). Excess glue which squeezes out from the ends may be smoothed off, to act as a fine filler between etch and plastic. The resulting glue bonds are very strong, with a degree of flexibility built in to cope with rough handling, derailments and the trials of exhibition use.

To complete work on the sides, fit a length of 10 by 60thou microstrip to the cantrail to represent the flexible weather strip located above the van doors. There is just enough plastic on the cantrail rainstrip to allow Mek Pak to form a bond.

The Hornby model does not have the deep headstocks (bufferbeams) characteristic of the prototype. Removing the strengthening ribs from the ends makes the van body too short as well. Careful observation of the prototype will show that the end bulkheads are substantial, with door stop detail in the corners. Make up new bulkheads from 40thou styrene sheet cut to 37mm by 33mm (to include the headstocks) with the top profiled to fit the roof and 1.5mm removed form the sides to represent the hinge recesses. The lack of deep headstocks on the Hornby model is to clear the tension lock couplings. If you require to use such couplings, then disregard the next steps...

Cut a piece of 20thou styrene card measuring 4.5mm by 31mm for each headstock, securing it into place with a drop of Mek Pak. They stand slightly proud of the end bulkhead. Once hardened, drill new holes, 1.5mm diameter, for the buffers, which may be original plastic mouldings or new turned brass Oleos from A1-Models. If you are considering the use of an AME underframe kit, then fit new bulkheads 33mm square and remove the headstocks completely (the underframe kit comes complete with headstocks and buffers of its own).

The original underframe is difficult to bring up to scratch because of the extent of the inaccuracy and its many compromises, but fine scale wheels, brake discs and disc brake callipers go a good way to enhance the final appearance. Hornby fit pivoting axleguards which are awkward to disguise and make three point compensation difficult to install. Fix the body to the original underframe moulding with spots of Araldite 'Rapid' if you have replaced the original buffers.

Finishing

At the very least, you should use good photographs of your chosen van prototype for reference, so that the correct positions of data panels and livery detail is possible. Numerous vans are to be found in faded and weathered Railfreight livery of rail red and Railfreight grey. A helpful innovation is the development of faded livery colours from Railmatch, absolutely ideal for modelling these vehicles. Only a few of them have made it into new livery schemes so use some weathered Rail red for a excellent base to apply weathering.

Vans regularly used for MOD traffic are normally found with a variety of HAZCHEM diamonds pasted to the doors. Some are applied on top of others as the loads have been changed and other unofficial markings are applied from time to time.

Thoroughly prime any brass with etching primer (nasty stuff - beware, and ensure good ventilation) to ensure that the paint gets a good key. I generally spray Rail red all over the body, then mask off for the Railfreight grey panels. Railmatch 'roof dirt' colour is a firm favourite for van roofs as well as coaching stock.

Decals are applied before a protective coat of matt varnish is applied. Weathering consists more of faded and patched paint rather than layers of brake dust, grime and rust, so make up some paint patches by spraying different shades of livery colours into decal film, and apply in the same manner as waterslide transfers.

Going the Extra Mile

Paradoxically, the conversion to the VAA, VBA and VCA variants of the standard airbraked van suddenly makes the underframe pattern supplied by Hornby technically correct, though its poor visual appearance is a problem for many modellers. At the time of writing, a simple way round the problem was available. Simply order spare VDA van bodies and obtain one of the two airbraked underframe kits from Appleby Model Engineering. Use kit No.4U05 for the VAA, VBA and VCA van type (which may be used under the Hornby OAA body too) and kit No.4U02 for the VDA van. This combination makes for quite inexpensive projects complete with accurate underframes.

Assemble the underframe kit fixed (or 'solid') or modify the underframes with

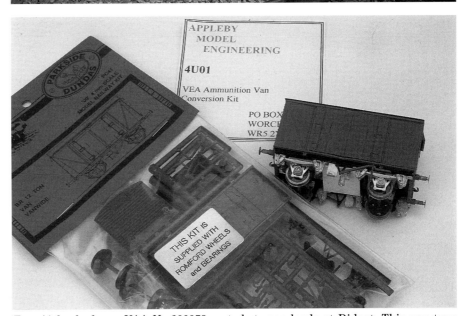

Top. Airbraked van VAA No.200079 rests between loads at Didcot. This van type sees frequent use on MOD traffic and as barrier wagons to protect locomotives from dangerous loads. August 1997.

Middle. Not a van specifically but details of suspensions fitted to 'standard' wagons refurbished for MOD use. This ZDA (ex-ODA) was refurbished with the same suspension as the VEA vans. Use these photographs to help you place the correct suspension detail on a VEA van model. Warrington, July 1997.

Bottom. Modelling VEA ammunition vans from the excellent Parkside Dundas vanwide kit is straightforward using the AME conversion kit.

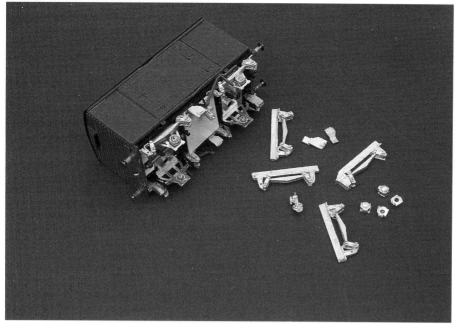

A completed underframe and the parts laid out for inspection. Fit the suspension parts to compensation W irons if you can; much more reliable running will be the result.

a MJT internal compensation unit. The number of good castings in each pack and the overall weight of white metal used in their manufacture makes the AME kit very good value for money. Detailed notes on assembly may be found in Chapter 2.

A common feature of all underframe kits from Appleby Model Engineering is the casting of axleguards and solebars as one unit. This is a similar arrangement to that found in ready to run underframes, so the best method of installing compensation is to use an inside bearing rocking unit. MJT manufactures an excellent system which is easy to use and fits the AME underframes perfectly. Perhaps the most difficult is the first of the two underframes described above, 4U05, which requires the inner frame to be trimmed, in order to make room for the compensation unit. Otherwise, modellers familiar with normal compensation axleguard sets will find the inner compensation units simple to fit; the only difference is the dismantling of one wheel set, filing off the axle points and then reassembling the wheel set to the compensation unit.

The inner bearings are etched with holes to accept the standard 2mm diameter axle as supplied with most wheelsets. A tiny spot of cyanoacrylate adhesive is all you need to fix the compensation assembly to the model floor. See Chapter 2 for principles of compensation.

Reassembly

In the case of all van models using AME underframe kits, the headstocks are removed flush with the bottom edge of the van sides. With detailing and finishing work completed, a floor measuring 29 by 130mm is cut from a sheet of 40thou styrene. Fit it to the inside of the van body, supported with offcuts of 40thou styrene glued into the van ends. The painted and finished underframe may be attached to this floor with a couple of tiny spots of Araldite.

VAA, VBA and VCA vans are the easiest to secure to the underframe because of the large inner frame casting. The VDA van requires a little more care in assembly because the only body locating points are the two frame spacers, situated towards the centre of the van.

Wheels

The standard AB vans are all disc braked, with a brake calliper bearing onto each wheel. Choice of wheels is left to the modeller, depending on the chosen gauge. Eight separate brake discs per van are required, fitted to each wheel and each side of the wheel. MJT supply etched nickel silver brake discs which fit most types of 12mm freight wagon wheel.

Middle. **Getting close! A complete and painted VEA shows some of the HAZCHEM panels that may be applied from the 'Lineside Look' transfer packs.**

Left. **A peek at the underside shows compensation W irons fitted with 10BA studding, and nuts providing the rocking axis.**

AIRBRAKED VANWIDES

Number Sequence	Date	Lot	Works
VEA Variants:			
230000-230049	1978	3918	Ashford
ZRA Departmental			
230050-230109	1981		Horwich
VFA ZRA/ZSA			
230110-230399	1982-3	4017	Horwich
VFA/ZRA/ZSA			
230400-230549	1983-4	4028	Shildon

ZRA/ZSA. Numbers: 230000-2, 230005, 230011, 230014, 230017, 230018, 230020, 230021, 230023, 230024, 230029, 230107, 230311, 230324-326, 230377 coded VFA, with translucent roof.
Original TOPS codes:
VEV vanwide with roller bearings
VMV vanwide with plain bearings in MOD traffic
VWV vanwide with plain bearings

The Hornby vans have come in from the cold a little since the introduction of underframe kits and other detailing parts. Once primed and painted, the underframes have the feel and appearance of a solid piece of railway engineering. A touch of dry brush weathering will bring out all that lovely cast detail. So go and take another look at those humble Hornby vans!

Airbraked Vanwides VEA and VFA

The classification 'Vanwides' was applied in pre-TOPS days because of the wide 9ft. door opening. Technically this wagon is the forerunner to the modern designs seen today - the VGA, ferry vans and the standard AB vans. Emphasis is on ease of unloading of payload using fork lift trucks, a piece of equipment common on today's railway.

Constructed to diagram 1/217 for palletised traffic, vanwides have sliding doors mounted on runners at roof and solebar level. They were a great success, with 2,000 entering traffic. Experimental translucent roofs to improve lighting for loading were fitted to Lot 3421, introducing an interesting variant to the family. Early features included heavy duty buffers, instanter couplings, oil axleboxes and 8 shoe clasp vacuum brakes. Buffers were replaced with Oleo versions with longer shank. As a result, coupling hooks had to be lengthened, with a welded steel fillet. The introduction of Speedlink and long wheelbase airbraked vans found all manner of standard designs (vanwides, palvans, shocvans etc.) withdrawn and broken up. The legacy of this remains, with redundant bodies littering farmyards, builders yards and so on, serving as steadily rotting stores and field shelters. A reprieve was in sight for some vanwides because sharp curves in some MOD sites were not ideal for long wheelbase vehicles. Refurbishment commenced for 550 vehicles, a project which included updated underframes and airbrakes.

Left and below. A complete model of a VCA van ready for service. The cast metal underframe matches this body very well. We will explore further uses for this underframe in Chapter 7. Railmatch produce faded paints suitable for this type of project and these may be used, before weathering and patch painting a model.

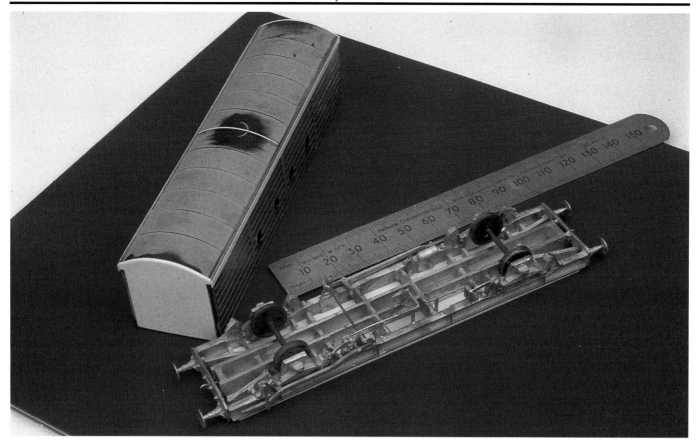

Modellers wanting one of the earlier 20ft. 9in. WB airbraked vans may use a donor model from Hornby, replacement brass sides from A1-Railmatch and an underframe kit from AME. Modifications to the body include removal of the roof ventilator and addition of van end bulkhead. To accommodate the new underframe the headstocks are removed from the van body.

'FAT 19' friction link suspension was installed to permit operation up to 75mph in Speedlink formations. They are numbered in the airbraked series and TOPS coded VEA/VFA. Delivered in freight bauxite brown, the standard livery of Railfreight grey and red soon dominated. Nearly all of the vanwides are now gone, though a handful remain in departmental use as brake force runners. Their demise came during the early 1990s as some MOD sites were closed.

Modelling

Hornby must be commended for producing an acceptable version of the vanwide, at least so far as the body is concerned. Critics spoke of inaccurate underframes and a body slightly short for this prototype but we had little else to work on so it sufficed. Parkside Dundas now produce a simple kit of the vanwide in plastic, released in 1993. The underframe as supplied is for vacuum braked wagons, making it difficult for modern image modellers to tackle a VEA.

Appleby Model Engineering produce a conversion pack to model VEAs and ODAs from the Parkside Dundas pipe wagon. (The ODA is a similar rebuild for MOD use and may be tackled using the same techniques as VEAs). Kit No.4U01 contains white metal castings for the axle boxes, suspension and airbrake equipment, which means that accurate underframe detail is possible. I'd recommend using MJT BR W iron axleguards to replace the plastic ones from the kit. The whole project is very simple and may be completed structurally in one after-

noon, providing you don't flood the plastic kit with solvent...

1. Following the instructions, assemble the Parkside kit body with Mek Pak solvent, noting how well the body fits together at the corners and roof. The underframe parts must be left alone at this point. Once the body is stable, remove all plastic from the underside of the floor without damaging the headstocks. Before fitting the roof, drill venting holes

in the floor and stick some ballast weight into the van body.

2. Carefully remove all axleguard and axlebox detail from the solebars. Clean and assemble the solebars to the wagon floor using MJT etched compensation axleguards as spacers. (Note that the bufferbeams are integral with the van ends). Compensation is easy to install (See Chapter 2), for the axleguards accept new axleboxes and suspensions from AME with ease. I trimmed some of the

As a simple detailing project, the Hornby VDA van is ideal and topical because of its revival during the mid-1990s. This model is painted in Railmatch faded rail red and features an underframe from AME.

white metal from the rear of the cast FAT 19 suspension units to ensure the compensation rocking unit worked well.
3. Complete the underframe by clipping in a set of three hole disc wheels, using them to align the eight brake shoes. Fit the air cylinder, brake levers and air distributor as the final parts.
4. Fine detailing of the model may include Roco air pipes and MJT coupling hooks, unless working screw couplings are fit ted.

Finishing
The livery notes are effectively the same for VEAs as for the larger Railfreight vans described earlier. If anything, the VEAs are plastered with more notices and HAZCHEMS than their larger brethren; weathering consists of peeled paint, rust and brake dust, but don't overdo it.

Above. **Underframe kits by AME have complete castings for solebars and axleguards. This is in a similar vein to many ready to run models. This VDA van is fitted with an MJT internal compensation rocking unit, in the same manner as ready to run models. Wheels are fitted with brake discs from the same source.**

Below. **VCA van in traffic on my layout 'Mitcham'.**

The A1-Railmatch kits are designed to be basic. You obtain what detail you want to finish the kit. This is a departmental YAA modelled from the Bogie Bolster D kit using Mendip Bogies and extra small details, like square section brass rod for stanchions, styrene for strap tensioners and styrene strip for a load, suitably printed.

A typical partner to the BDA/YAA bolster wagons, a runner wagon to accommodate overlength loads. Pipes, steel bars and rail are typical of 'out of gauge' loads. This is a white metal kit from AME.

CHAPTER FOUR
Some Projects for Steel

Most wagons built to carry steel are bogie types with adaptations to accommodate various forms of unfinished and semi finished steel products. Traffic is diverse and expanding under the auspices of EWS - an entire book could be devoted to this freight and its wagons alone...

Modern steel wagons are well represented in 4mm scale, and a choice may be made immediately from the following:

BAA: Airbraked bogie bolster used on cold reduced (CRC) and hot rolled coil (HRC), blooms, slab etc. Available as a plastic kit from Cambrian Models. Coil cradles are not included in the kit.

BBA: Airbraked bogie bolster used on similar traffics as the BAA. Many are rebuilt into different forms for conveying HRC and CRC in box cradles to prevent damage. Cambrian Models produce a basic plastic kit, but coil cradles are not included.

BQW: Vacuum braked bogie bolster C used during the early 1990s for pipe traffic to and from Hartlepool. The wagons operated to Leith Docks (Edinburgh) with pipes for the oil industry. The wagons were modified with special bolsters for both untreated steel and coated pipes. The basic model is available from Bachmann, but the modeller will need to enhance it with Gloucester bogies and vacuum brake detail.

BDA: Bogie bolster D is a design utilised intensively on general steels and owes Railfreight/EWS little. Many are scheduled for early replacement after a hard life on primary steel traffic from South Wales, Sheffield, Scunthorpe, Tees-side and Longport. The old Civil Link network utilised a large number for transporting finished rail from Workington in conjunction with runner wagons. The BDA bogie bolster wagons were rebuilt from various forms in the early 1980s with airbrakes and Y25C bogies. This form is available from Cambrian models as a plastic kit. A1-Railmatch produce a brass kit for the BDA which excludes bogies. Bogies may be obtained from Mendip Models or AME.

YLA/YQA Borail: Two basic forms, a bolster wagon used for finished rail from Workington (TOPS YLA Carkind Mullet) and a modified Borail (TOPS YQA Carkind Parr) for new sleepers. All are refurbished vehicles with airbrakes and Y25C bogies. A1-Railmatch produce a basic kit for the Borail in etched brass, in a similar format to the BDA. Y25C bogies can be got from Mendip Models or AME.

SPA 2 axle plate wagon: Constructed in large numbers and modified to several specialised forms for carrying wire. Cambrian Models produce a basic plastic kit which may be enhanced with underframe parts from Mendip Models. An interesting enhancement is the hood to make a SEA variant. This is available from AME as a resin casting. Sadly the prototypes have lost the hoods, though they still feature the structural modifications.

RNA 2 axle runner wagon: Designed for use between BDA and YLA wagons when carrying over-length rail or bar. Most runner wagons are stripped down revenue vehicles such as vans and opens, using some of the underframes described in Chapter 2. AME produce a white metal kit of one type, based on a VDA van underframe.

Unfortunately some of the more interesting prototypes are not available for 4mm modellers. The characteristic telescopic hood wagons used on European traffic as

Runner wagon and Bogie Bolster D together in departmental yellow grey livery. To create a patched or faded livery, just add a touch of white to the paint colour. Many wagons become faded rather than dirty.

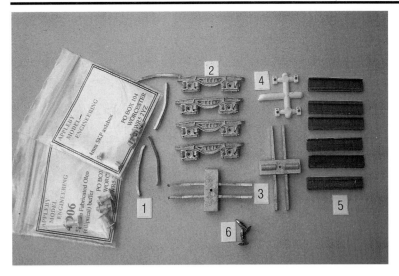

well as some internal flows are sold as HO scale models at 3.5mm to 1 foot, but not in 4mm. Some 18 metre ferry wagons are also used on steel traffic, but the same scale restriction applies. Models of both are made by Roco. Scratchbuilding remains the only method to obtain models of the continental types, involving complex styrene techniques.

Modelling

The two bogie bolster kits from A1 Railmatch are the subjects for this Chapter; the BDA bogie bolster D and the YLA Borail, they are typical vehicles used throughout the main line network for steel traffic. Etched brass is an ideal medium for such models, for it will not sag or warp like models constructed from styrene plastic (if it is not braced adequately). You have to get the small details to complete the kits, such as Y25C bogies, Oleo buffers, airtanks, airpipes and air distributors. A1 Railmatch do include cast bolsters in both kits, however.

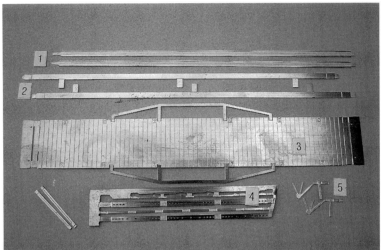

Top left. Essential bits and pieces for both BDA bogie bolsters and the Borail wagons. 1 Bogie frame linkages, curved in shape; 2 Fabricated Y25 bogie sideframes from AME; 3 Bogie inner frames; 4 Cosmetic tail lamps - a nice finishing touch by Replica Railways; 5 Cast metal bolsters. Also shown are alternative axleboxes for the bogies and elliptical buffers from AME.

Middle left. The basic parts to the Bogie Bolster D kit produced by A1-Railmatch. All the parts are etched in brass which makes a very strong wagon when soldered together. The main floor unit (3) is folded into shape; the sides (2) and solebars (1) are soldered into place. The kit comes with cast bolsters and may be adapted to one of a variety of forms based on the Bogie Bolster D-format. A1-Railmatch do not supply bogies: they are available from Mendip Models or AME for the airbraked wagons or AME and Ratio for pre-1980 unrefurbished versions.

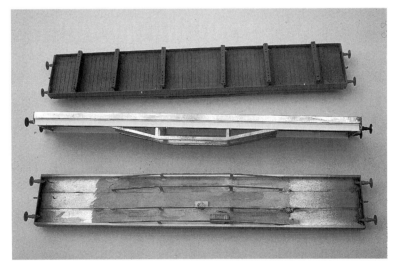

Left. Bogie Bolster D models in various stages of assembly. The etched solebar may be replaced with Evergreen Styrene 4mm channel. Small details to be fitted include an air tank, airbrake distributor, truss rod bracing and round freight Oleo buffers from A1-Railmatch. Styrene card is ideal for making suitable loads: two pieces of 100thou styrene cut to 209mm by 115mm makes convincing slab when painted in dull silver and dusted with dark rust.

Bottom. Parts for the basic A1-Railmatch Borail kit. This folds and solders together in a similar manner to the Bogie Bolster D kit. The floor unit (1) folds together, but I find it more authentic to remove the fish belly and solder them on separately, slightly inboard of the floor. This is enhanced by the frame (2) and the sides. The sides themselves may be modified by cutting in the slots for tensioners. Also shown are buffers from AME (3), Y25 bogies (4) and the load bolsters (5). If you are modelling a YQA Parr, do not fit the fixed bolsters. This wagon type is equipped with lengthwise strips of timber to support loads of pre-cast concrete sleepers.

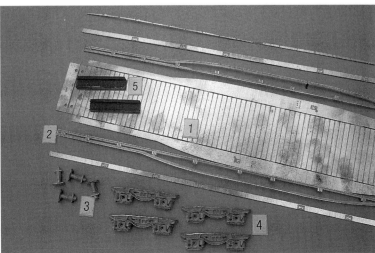

Type	TOPS	No Sequence	Variants
Bogie Bolster D	BDA	950201-900	BFA with 4
	YAA	with gaps	fixed bolsters
	BMA	From same sequence	Fixed ends
	BDA	950901-951250	
	BFA	with gaps	

All were initially refurbished (1979-81) from unfitted/vacuum braked bogie bolster Ds to modern airbraked vehicles with Y25C bogies.

Borail	YLA	DC967500-649	YQA

YLA: Mullet. Bolster wagon for carrying rail.

YQA: Parr Flat wagon for carrying sleepers.

All initially refurbished in 1981-2 as life extension with Y25C bogies and Airbrakes.

Above. Bogie Bolster D, YNA No.KDC950756 was parked at Exeter Riverside Yard in September 1996. Note the odd axleboxes on the fabricated Y25 bogie.

Left. Bogie Bolster D. A YAA, coded Brill, No.950129 at Newport in September 1996. This is a typical example, with six fixed bolsters and fabricated Y25 bogies. The load is steel bars from Tremorfa steelworks in Cardiff. The livery is faded and patched departmental yellow and grey. Many former revenue wagons transferred to departmental use are being returned to front line duties by EWS.

Below. An end view of YNA No.KDC950756. The bogies are fitted with characteristic curved linkages on the ends and clasp brakes. This wagon is missing its stanchions from the bolsters. Round Oleo buffers are fitted, in common with the rest of the BDA fleet.

This example typifies the Sheerness Steel hired PXAs (this one is still coded POA). PXA (POA) No.PR3132 features Schlieren bogies, a heavily ribbed body which extends to the headstocks and a scratched weathered livery of light blue. Sheerness, November 1993.

PXA No.PR3156, made of underframe components recovered from redundant TEA tank wagons.

CHAPTER FIVE
Private Owner Scrap Wagon Projects

Scrap metal traffic has produced a variety of different private owner airbraked wagons in the last fifteen years. This business is still active today, with flows to Sheerness, Cardiff and Aldwarke, near Rotherham. Wagons constructed for such a material are essentially heavily reinforced boxes, riding either on two axle underframes or on bogies.

PROJECT 1
Steel by the Sea in Sheerness
Co Steel Sheerness Ltd (formerly Sheerness Steel Co. Ltd.) is a prominent customer of Trainload Freight/EWS, with a fleet of bogie box wagons for the collection of scrap steel to feed the furnaces at the Sheerness site. Only recently have the familiar blue box bogie scrap wagons bearing the legend 'Sheerness Steel' been replaced by a new design of vehicle, bringing an era to a close on the Sheppey line so far as freight traffic is concerned. My interest spanned the years from 1985 to about 1994, an interest which included the former Sheerness Steel PXA/JXA wagons and my various efforts to scratchbuild them.

The Appleby Model Engineering (AME) catalogue includes a comprehensive kit for one of the Sheerness Steel prototypes. Modellers who find modern rail wagons of interest will be quick to point out the differences between various batches of these vehicles and that the AME kit is based on one of four wagon types at one time hired by Sheerness Steel.

Historical and Technical Details for Modelling
The concept of high capacity scrap steel wagons was extensively tested by the conversion of the diagram 6/455 PXA finished steel bogie bolsters. This was considered a success, and the 16t mineral wagon fleet previously used was replaced by modern PXA wagons built by Procor at Wakefield and leased to Sheerness Steel during the 1980s. This fleet of forty wagons was supplemented by additional batches of PXA vehicles rebuilt on redundant TEA 102t tank wagon underframes. Many varied in their external appearance, much to the delight of enthusiasts who could count on some interesting formations on the Sheppey branch.

Initially, the PXAs travelled far and wide, collecting scrap from various metal recycling companies and returning to Sheerness in the (then) numerous Speedlink services. A series of local trip workings to and from Ridham Dock on a daily basis offered employment for these distinctively liveried vehicles, collecting metal from the car fragmentation works located in the dock estate. The demise of Speedlink reduced the sphere of operation to a regular block train working of scrap steel from Snailwell and Meyer Parry at Willesden - the only significant traffic worked to the Isle of Sheppey. Some of the PXA wagons were stored until the complete withdrawal of the PXA fleet from scrap steel traffic in 1995 and some of the PR3100-3139 PXAs found themselves rebuilt with removable covers, for a new role in semi-finished steel traffic originating from South Wales. Others are used for spoil traffic.

New wagons have been introduced in the last few years, rebuilds of bogie coil hood wagons originally built in 1986-88 by Powell Duffryn. The conversion work was undertaken by RFS at Doncaster, replacing the flexure hood with new rigid sides and ends reinforced with very substantial ribs. The origin of these vehicles is clearly indicated by the distinctive underframe design and the use of Gloucester GPS bogies. These vehicles are TOPS coded JXA in the number sequence (with gaps) TIPH 3008-3062.

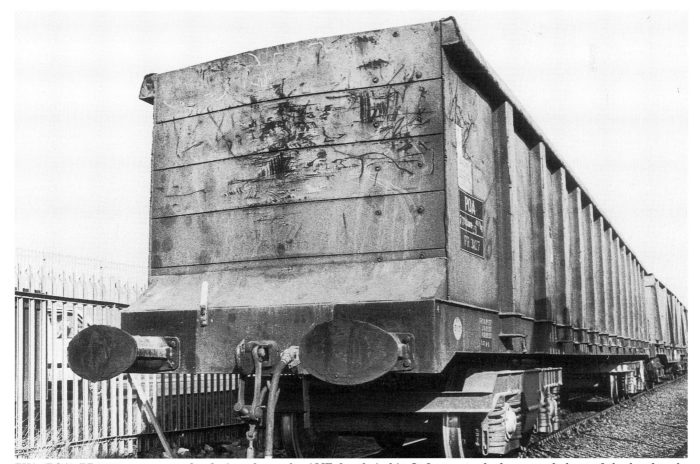

PXA (POA) PR3107 represents the design chosen by AME for their kit. It features a body stopped short of the headstocks, with an angle plate fitted to prevent the take-up of scrap particles on the short platform. The plugs are all that remain of the ladder.

To Summarise:

PXA PR3000 to PR3007. Design codes JX030C and JX030B. Built in 1974-75, the finished steel wagons were converted to PXA scrap carriers as prototypes. Careful observation of this small batch of vehicles shows some small structural variations. For example, PR3000 has a different end and side rib arrangement to PR3001, so modellers are advised to use good photographs of any vehicle they are proposing to model. The bogie type was the Gloucester Clasp MK2 available from AME in 4mm scale. The wagons are characterised by fishbelly underframes and diagonal bracing ribs on the wagon sides. With an overall length of 55 feet, they are shorter than later batches of wagons built for this traffic. Scratchbuilding from styrene card is the only way of obtaining a suitable model to represent this batch of wagons.

PXA TIPH 3008-3062 with gaps. Recent conversions of former Powell Duffryn flexure hood bogie coil wagons to scrap carriers for Co Steel Sheerness Ltd. Liveried in Tiphook dark blue livery. The only method of obtaining a model of this vehicle is to scratchbuild the body from styrene card and strip, using GPS bogies from AME.

PXA PR3100 TO PR3129. Design Code JX029A. The first production batch of Sheerness Steel wagons, a design distinguished by a body slightly shorter than the underframe. The AME kit represents this batch (AME rightly selecting the commonest wagon from this traffic base). Technical details include Schlieren M25 bogies, Blair pattern buffers and airbrake equipment. Many have access ladders installed both on the outer end and in the diagonally opposite corners, to assist with cleaning out. Opposite corners are fitted with angle plates to prevent excessive build up of scrap debris in the wagon body.

The prototype measures 62ft.7in. in length over buffers, which equates to a length of 250mm in 4mm scale. Body height is 6ft.3in. or 25mm in 4mm scale. The body supplied by AME matches this exactly when fitted with the cast white metal buffers supplied in the kit.

PXA PR3130-3139. Design code JX029B. The same as above except the body, which is the same length as the underframe. All other details match the vehicle described above, but building a model means scratchbuilding the body. Schlieren bogies may be obtained from both AME and Mendip Models. Bogie kits from Mendip Models are slightly different in cosmetic detail and completely different in terms of bogie spacer detail.

PXA PR3140-49. Design Code PX029C. This is a small batch of PXAs hired to Sheerness Steel after becoming redundant from Foster Yeoman aggregate traffic. Built using running gear from redundant TEA 102t tank wagons to a length of 53ft.1in., equating to 212mm over buffers in 4mm scale. These former aggregate wagons had slightly lower sides to those in the next batch, built to design code PX029D. The only option is to scratchbuild from styrene utilising detailing parts from AME and A1 Railmatch. *(cont. on page 37)*

Top. PXA (POA) PR3132, with remnant stumps of its end access ladder. The body is extended to the headstocks on this wagon.

Middle. PXA (POA) PR3003 is a rebuild from one of the original finished steel carriers. The body patterns vary between nearly all of the original wagons of this type, so beware...

Bottom. Prior to the introduction of Tiphook Rail JXA bogie box wagons a number of ex-TML JXA wagons underwent trials with Sheerness Steel.

Inspiration in Colour

Inspiration for a model can come from unexpected quarters; a chance photograph of a single vehicle or new products from trade sources. Discovery of a certain diameter plumber's pipe opened up a huge range of possibilities for me. I have never looked at a DIY shop in the same way since. The efforts of other modellers can be a motivating force too: if *he* can build it, so can I. The following photographs will, I hope, provide some ideas and thoughts on possible projects, both simple and complex.

Above. Telescopic hood wagons may be purchased as rtr models in HO scale. They look fine until you couple them to 4mm scale British outline stock, when their small size becomes apparent. The other option is to scratchbuild from 60 and 80thou styrene sheet and Evergreen styrene strip and fit bogie kits from AME. The result is satisfying, but this is some project to undertake - each wagon has nearly 100 ribs to cut and fit.

Below. Depressed centre ECC china clay slurry tanks are modelled from 32mm diameter pipe, with cast ends from Mendip Models. Ladders and walkways are from A1-Railmatch packs, while transfers are taken from Craftsman and Fox transfers. The underframe may be modelled from fine styrene strip and 4mm channel because the pipe is so rigid. Bogie mounting screws are fixed directly into the tank itself. Small fittings are a mixture of styrene detail and parts from various manufacturers.

Above. If sufficient bracing is provided, styrene may be used to build large, complex vehicles without distortion, such as this Polybulk. Fox Transfers produce the markings for this powder hopper type and grainflow polybulks too. When scratchbuilding, take advantage of all of the available parts from the trade, to save time and effort.

Below. Example of what may be achieved using ready to run products. The Seacows are from Lima, enhanced with etched details and welded ribs to represent examples built from 1981. The Gunnell is a rebuild from a Lima PGA hopper wagon, using etched brass detail from A1-Railmatch.

Above. A complex proposition is the ECC/Tiphook Rail Clay Tiger. This model was made using 35mm diameter waste pipe from a plumber's merchant. It was cut to length and then cut in half down its length. The rest is a simple styrene structure built for rigidity onto a floor of 80thou styrene. Styrene card may be curved by forming it over an appropriate surface after immersion in nearly boiling water. This technique has limitations and is only appropriate to fairly simple curvatures. In this case, it's much easier to use a plastic pipe instead.

Below. Simple kits like the Dace ballast wagon from AME can help a modeller populate his freight yard quite quickly. Notice the 'ghost' around the transfers and lettering blocks. This is annoying but may be avoided by coating the wagon in gloss varnish before applying transfers. Once the transfers are dry, recoat the model in matt varnish.

Above. This is an elegant project, ideal for adding a little something to a layout. The basic wagon is a Cambrian Kits SPA plate wagon kit enhanced with Mendip Models axleguards and A1-Railmatch freight Oleo buffers. To convert the SPA into an SEA hooded wagon, add the AME resin flexible hood. This is painted separately, before gluing into place. AME produce the transfers too.

Below. Sheerness Steel PXA, built from another AME kit, painted and finished with AME transfers and paints. Weathering colours are available from Railmatch as light rust and dark rust. These basic colours may be enhanced and shaded subtly, by mixing in tiny quantities of rail red and yellow.

Above. Use a Hornby PGA aggregate hopper to model this prototype. PGA No.PR14445 stands at Didcot in July 1997.

Below. Lima have produced a basic model for this prototype. Some enhancement is needed around the underframe and the bogies on the model are not correct. The prototype is represented by Croxton and Garry JCA No.CG 9550 at Workington in August 1995.

Above. Fans of the Mendip stone traffic will be pleased with the available kits from Mendip Models, for various large bogie wagons operated from Merehead and Whatley. ARC bogie hopper ARC 17914 is an 'outer wagon' fitted with conventional draw gear on one end. ARC paint colours are produced by Railmatch, transfers by Fox.

Below. Former BSC iron ore tipplers are also used on Mendip stone traffic. JUA No.PR 26242 may be modelled from kits by AME and Mendip Models. The JUA bogie box wagons are also classified as 'outer' or 'inner' depending upon the draw gear arrangements.

Some detail for the discerning modeller. PXA No.PR3103 shows end access door detail and the way the body stops short of the headstocks on many of the prototypes. The side door permits entry to the wagon body, for cleaning and maintenance.

(cont. from page 30)
PXA PR3150-59. Design Code PX029D. Built in 1986 by Procor, these wagons take a similar profile to those described previously, with parts recovered from old tank wagons. They feature Gloucester bogies and a large box body similar to that on PXAs PR3130-39. These vehicles are (incorrectly) documented as being 53ft.1in. in length over buffers too, but the correct dimension is as given earlier, 62ft.7in. Body height is 6ft.3in., or 25mm in 4mm scale. Like the earlier batches, the wagons are equipped with internal and external ladders (nearly all missing by now), airbrakes and rugged external ribs.

In order to complete the picture, it is worth mentioning other bogie box wagons used by Sheerness Steel. A set of three KEA wagons were trailed as a possible replacement for existing PXAs. Rebuilt flexurehood wagons were chosen instead and the rest, as they say, is history. *(Note-*

This wagon type has to resist a rain of knocks and bashes from loading and unloading the scrap steel.

Underframe detail of PXA PR3152; components are recovered from ex-TEA 102t tank wagons. This vehicle has Gloucester bogies.

Complex data panels are applied to the solebar as well as the wagon body. A close up view of a Gloucester bogie and clasp brakes on PR3151.

Schlieren M25 bogies feature on most of the PR 3100-3139 wagons. Note that the angled end faces 'outwards', towards the headstock. The nearest wheel is fitted with a brake disc.

TOPS code PXA was later changed to JXA - hence design codes with JXxxx letters are still branded PXA.)

Kit Building
The Appleby Model Engineering kit for design code PX029A is simple to construct despite the size of the vehicle. As I cleaned the moulding pipes from the solebar and bogie bearing pads, I thought, not for the first time, that this is not a wagon for small layouts. Its simplicity derives from the superbly cast resin body which leaves little for the modeller to do except add some external detailing. All these, including airtank, brake distributor buffers and angleplates, are faithfully cast in white metal. The bogies supplied are Schlieren M25 type cast in white metal complete with a nicely executed brake wheel for each. Mounting for the bogie is achieved with an 8BA studding tapped into the

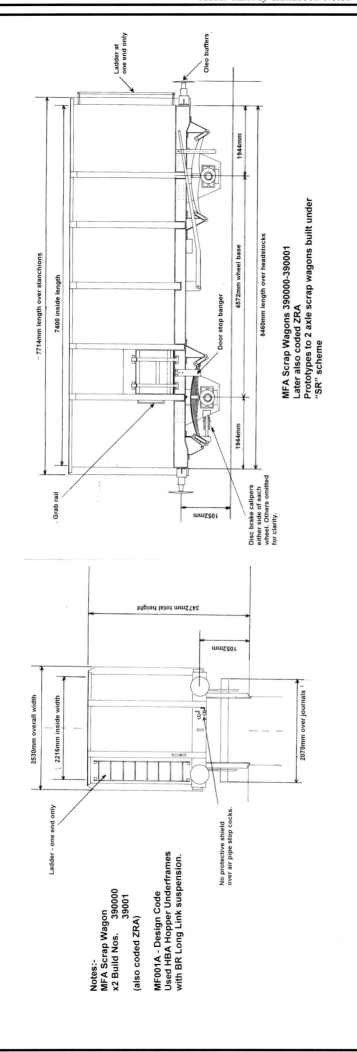

MFA Scrap Wagons 390000-390001
Later also coded ZRA
Prototypes to 2 axle scrap wagons built under
"SR" scheme

Notes:-
MFA Scrap Wagon
x2 Build Nos.   390000
                390001
(also coded ZRA)

MF001A - Design Code
Used HBA Hopper Underframes
with BR Long Link suspension.

underside of the body, on which the bogies may freely pivot.

Commence construction by cleaning the resin body of rough mould lines, moulding pips and burrs with a scalpel. The top lip of the body needs a gentle rub with grade 800 wet and dry paper before washing in soapy water to remove contamination from casting processes (as advised in the assembly instructions). Add the various details and studding using Araldite 'Rapid' - assembly is a swift process, taking less than fifteen minutes to complete.

If you fancy your chances at a little scratchbuilding, then a PR3150-59 series PXA is a good candidate. I have built seven of these vehicles and three of the PR3130-39 series PXAs, from Evergreen styrene card. The techniques are more or less the same whichever wagon you choose to build, but if you are really keen then batch build them in multiples of three or four. This is easier than you may think, because it takes little more time to cut six or eight body sides from 40thou styrene than it takes to cut two. Whilst you are set up for the two, then just keep going. You may wish to obtain the following detailing components for your scratchbuilding effort:
Airbrake tanks from A1-Railmatch.
Air brake distributors from AME.
Gloucester bogies from AME.
Buffers from either AME or A1-Railmatch.
0.45mm Brass wire. Eileen's Emporium.
Brake wheels. Etched in brass from A1-Railmatch.
Coupling hooks from MJT.
Bogie spacers from A1-Railmatch (optional component to assist assembly of the bogies).
Transfers for Sheerness Steel livery produced and sold by AME.
Top hat bearings of 2mm diameter from Romford or Kean Maygib.

Assemble as follows:
1. Cut the body sides from 40thou styrene measuring 198mm by 25mm, and ends to 31mm by 25mm, ensuring that all burrs are removed with wet and dry paper. Cut the floor from 80thou styrene, measuring 198mm by 29mm. Assemble the bogies on a flat sheet of plate glass which will help keep everything square. Leave the assembled bodies for at least 24 hours to harden sufficiently to take rough handling.

2. Add the vehicle solebars, measuring 200mm in length by 4mm deep cut from 40thou styrene card. Fit a top rib to the body from 40thou square strip and then leave to harden. Follow up with the body strengthening ribs which are, it must be said, a bit of a slog for more than one wagon. Cut them to a length of 24mm; a total of 26 ribs per wagon is required. Please note that the inner 11 ribs are evenly spaced, the outer pair are spaced differently. I used photographs to gauge the spacing as accurately as possible, ensuring all are added to the model as square as possible. Take your time over this particular job as any misaligned ribs will stick out like the proverbial sore thumb.

Two models of Sheerness Steel PXAs. The one in the foreground is built from the AME kit and the one beyond is scratchbuilt, with the body extended to the headstocks.

3. That completes the body structure, leaving only the small details. Profile the top rib to an angle as seen on all of the PR31XX series wagons. There is an inspection hatch at the far right end of each side, and this may be represented by a square of 10thou styrene, 7mm by 7mm. Add hinges and bolt detail, from scraps of styrene rod and strip from a Slaters mixed microstrip pack. The headstocks are cut from 20thou styrene, measuring 1.5mm deeper than the solebars and 31mm in length. Before fitting this de-

tail, drill holes to accept buffers and a single air pipe. Other fine details include the plates situated at the base of the strengthening ribs and fitting of the end hand rungs. Install angleplates to the inside corners of the body.

4. Fit MJT or AME oval buffers to the headstocks, along with a coupling hook and the single air pipe. I use those produced by Details West or Roco, which are primarily intended for the American/Continental HO scene.

5. At one time, finding the right bogies was almost impossible, however the Gloucester bogies appropriate to this model *are* available. They are assembled in the same manner as the AME bogies described in Chapter 2. They too may be added to a brass bogie frame from A1-Railmatch, to make life a little easier.

Liveries
The livery carried by the Sheerness Steel PXAs is an attractive light blue, offset by dark blue solebars and headstocks. Exceptions are the new Tiphook owned vehicles which are an overall dark blue, including one which has a horizontal yellow stripe.

Paints for this and the Tiphook Rail livery may be obtained direct from AME. The original Sheerness Steel light blue is 'Arctic Blue' and 'Aircraft Blue' is the dark blue used on the underframes. JXAs are documented with two logos and company branding styles, both available from AME on one transfer sheet. Additional details may be obtained from Fox Transfers such as the Procor and Caib brandings as well as additional electrification warning flashes.

PROJECT 2
The Standard Railfreight Scheme
In 1976 BR produced two prototype two axle scrap wagons consisting of simple welded boxes on HEA type underframes, forerunners of the Standard Railfreight ('SR' for short) and RLS scrap wagons common today. Constructed at Shildon and coded MFA, both wagons featured airbrakes for integration into the Speedlink network. A pointer for the pri-

Phoenix Paints, marketed by AME, were used to finish the models. AME also market the transfers for both early and later lettering styles for Sheerness Steel Co. Weathering is a mixture of Railmatch dark and light rust leavened with spots of yellow, dry brushed over raised detail. Fine scratch lines are penned on and an overall dust of dark rust completes the picture.

'SR' POA wagons

Number	Date	Details
RLS 5900	1976	Prototype 2 axle wagon. 24ft 4 inch length
RLS5901-5920	1982	Modified body, 26ft 4inch length
RLS5921-5980	1984	New build with Gloucester suspension
RLS5000-5099	1984	Rebuild of former BSC PGA hoppers

vate wagon builders was a statement of policy to encourage PO fleets rather than leave it to Railfreight to supply wagons. The 'SR' fleet was constructed with financial assistance from a Section 8 grant. A complex leasing arrangement was arranged through Barclays Bank via Mercantile Credit. They were

Scratchbuilding bogie box wagons is an ideal way to exercise a few styrene techniques for the first time. This model consists of a simple box, ribbed with styrene strip from Evergreen and fitted with AME bogies.

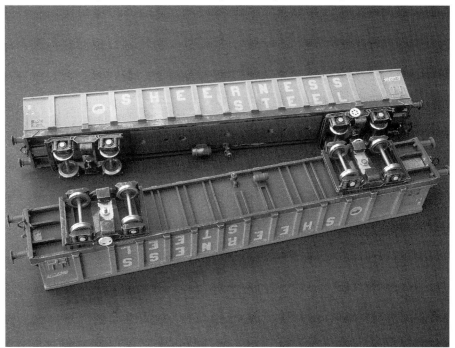

A view of the underside of both PXA models.

taken into BR ownership in 1990 and renumbered into the airbraked wagon sequences and coded SSA.

RLS 5900 was built by Standard Wagon under the 'SR' scheme as a prototype for evaluation. Featuring Gloucester floating suspension and rugged superstructure designed to withstand abuse, it proved successful in traffic, except for a certain weakness in the body design. The next batch of 20 wagons, RLS 5901-20, incorporated improvements over the prototype with extended underframe and improved body bracing.

A production run of 160 wagons of two designs soon followed. The first 100 had underframes from redundant PGA hopper wagons; the second 60 were built from new. Upon entering traffic, they replaced ageing 16t mineral wagons on scrap metal traffic in the South Yorkshire area.

Modelling
Cambrian produce a simple kit for the 160 production POA wagons while

One of the prototype POA wagons, rebuilt from a finished steel carrier. Bogies are Gloucester types from AME, buffers are MJT cast metal and the styrene is from Evergreen. Phoenix paint and AME transfers complete the picture.

New, out of the box and pristine model of a 'Standard Railfreight' POA from Bachmann. A perfect model for enhancement, weathering and beating up a little, but don't over do it. This model only represents the first 100 production wagons, rebuilt from redundant BSC PGA hoppers with BSC pedestal suspensions and stepped solebars. The pre-privatisation form is represented by the model; the former 'Standard Railfreight' fleet has been refurbished with new bodies.

In spite of the recent Bachmann release, modellers must not disregard the valuable Cambrian kit for the POA/SSA. It provides the means to model the last 60 production wagons which are different from the first 100 and offers lots of spare parts to model other POA wagons, such as my RLS POA (shown unpainted). The body is constructed from 40thou styrene and Evergreen Styrene ribs.

Bachmann have released an rtr model for the first production version.

The Cambrian kit represents the prototype 'as built', so modellers seeking to model EWS rebuilds will be faced with modifying the kit. It contains components for both types, moulded in light grey styrene plastic. Useful extra parts include airtanks, brake wheels and suspension units, all of which may also serve for other projects. The kit does not include parts such as overspill plates (located on the bodyside ribs) added during the service life of the vehicles.

Modellers may well wish to add extra parts, such as etched brass ladders, Oleo buffers turned in brass, styrene strip for deflection plates and compensation W irons to use as frames to mount the moulded suspension units. All complement it beautifully.

Begin construction with the body/floor sub-assembly, using sparing amounts of Mek Pak. Add the internal corner braces before leaving the model to harden for a couple of hours. Pare away plastic buffer webs from the headstocks and drill 1.0mm diameter holes for new Oleo buffers. Secure buffers with cyanoacrylate glue. The wagon floor is labelled to locate all the underframe detail correctly.

Replace the fold up plastic axleguards with etched brass axleguards (any type will do) for strength and accuracy. Fold them in the usual manner, either as solid frames or compensated. Don't fit to the wagon until the solebars are located.

RLS 5000-99 wagons are represented with stepped solebars and 4 spring BSC suspensions. The solebar fits to a lip on the floor so bracing ribs line up with those on the body. The kit allows enough room between solebars to fit brass axleguards/compensation units; be sure to align them correctly. Building a model from this batch leaves the straight solebar mouldings as spares, suitable for use in other projects. This is the version represented by the Bachmann model.

RLS 5921-80 wagons are not represented by Bachmann's rtr model and can only be derived from the Cambrian kit. They are constructed from the same superstructure parts supplied in the kit but the underframes require straight solebars and Gloucester suspension mouldings instead. Be aware of some small brake details between wagons.

Despite a change to BR ownership in 1990, the livery details remained unchanged until EWS ownership. The wagon ends are yellow, while sides, solebars and suspension units are blue (the same colour as Barclays Bank corporate blue). The well known 'SR' markings and TOPS panels are available from Cambrian dry print sheets whilst Railmatch produce the correct paint colours.

PROJECT 3
Other POA Scrap Wagons
Construction of scrap wagons did not stop at the Standard Railfreight designs. In

Standard Wagon POAs

TOPS	Number Seq.	Date	Code	Notes
POA	*RLS4560-79*	*1989*	*PO018A*	*Used former PEA frames*
POA	*RLS4585-90*	*1989*	*PO022B*	*Used former PMA frames*
POA	*RLS4591-95*	*1989*	*PO022C*	*Used former PRA frames*
POA	*RLS4596-4606*	*1989*	*PO022A/B*	*Used former PMA frames*
POA	*RLS4607*	*1989*	*PO010E*	*Used former PSA frame*
POA	*RLS4608*	*1989*	*PO022D*	*Used former PMA frame*
POA	*RLS5214-33*	*1987*	*PO018A*	*Used former PEA frames*

The Cambrian kit for the 'Standard Railfreight' wagon, complete but unpainted. It is modified with etched ladders and some angleplates fitted to horizontal ribs.

continued to build scrap wagons in the late 1980s for traffic to and from Allied Steel and Wire, Cardiff. Seven separate batches of 2 axlebox wagons (code POA) were built, with straight solebars and either BSC 4 spring or Gloucester suspensions.

Not all POAs still serve only for scrap and traffic has included lime, coal slurry and aggregates. Do not confuse this sequence with POA/PNA wagons, built for aggregate/potash/limestone traffic.

My interest in Standard Wagon's POA scrap wagons has centred around the RLS 4560-79 sequence of 1989. I used a basic 40thou styrene box measuring 104mm by 31mm by 28mm deep (outside dimensions allowing for 1mm styrene card thickness). Weld a lip of 60thou square styrene strip to the top of the sides and position it 1.5mm below the top edge of the body forming a recess, to be filled with Milliput filler. Once this is hard, profile the top edge to match that in the photographs, finishing with 800 grit wet and dry paper. Apply the remainder of the ribs using 40thou square styrene strip to the body ends and sides.

1988-89, Powell Duffryn introduced a fleet of 60 POAs (PDUF 4500-4559) which used redundant TTA underframes from the SUKO 612xx, 615xx, 617xx and 618xx number sequences. The body is a simple rugged design, ideal for scratchbuilding from styrene. Use an underframe kit from AME as a base for a body measuring 104mm by 33mm by 28mm deep. The Hornby underframe is useful but requires the same additional detailing as a TTA tank wagon - see Chapter 8 - to bring it up to scratch.

The Standard Wagon company

Use any remaining parts from a Cambrian POA kit (straight solebars, air tanks, disc brake calliper mouldings, set of suspension mouldings) to reduce the scratchbuilding element to a minimum. Cast white metal suspension details from AME; buffers and airtanks from A1-Railmatch; etched axleguards, disc brake inserts and coupling hooks from MJT will all enhance your model. Assemble the straight solebars to the wagon floor, using etched axleguards as spacers to ensure enough room for axleguard detail and wheels.

Cut new headstocks, 5mm by 32mm, from 40 thou styrene. Drill 1mm holes for buffers and coupling hook before fitting. Fit the etched axleguard frames, cosmetic axleguards and wheels, then the disc brake callipers to the inner wheelbase, along with

Kit and rtr model of the POA/SSA side by side.

airtank and brake wheels. Externally, small details such as deflector plates for end bracing and the centrally located access doors may be made up from styrene strips. I use the Slaters mixed pack and choose appropriate sizes for hinges and locking devices.

Livery Details

Both Powell Duffryn and Standard Wagon POAs are painted in black with hatched yellow/black lines on the top bracing rib. The black is extended to solebar and running gear on the Standard Wagon POAs. The twisted wire emblem is available as a transfer from AME, whilst TOPS panels may be taken from the Cambrian dry print sheet produced for their kits.

As far as weathering is concerned, the knocks taken during everyday operations are severe, usually from electromagnets or falling scrap. A courageous approach is to introduce gouges and dents using a temperature controlled soldering iron. Then paint the model in Railmatch dark rust with patches of light rust. Mask off small areas of the model with Humbrol Maskol (a liquid masking medium) before applying livery colours. Once dry, remove the Maskol by simply peeling it off, to reveal rust patches appearing from under the paint. Complete the livery details and weather with dilute washes of dark rust and dark grey paint.

POA RLS4562 at Sheerness Steel Works in 1992. A type very rarely seen at this location, I can only assume it was there for load trials. Note the heavily ribbed body, BSC suspensions and straight solebars. This may be modelled from parts taken from the Cambrian kit, with A1-Railmatch buffers and styrene card for the superstructure. AME have recently added this vehicle to their range of wagon kits. "Black Adders".

Cambrian POA model posed beside an RLS design of POA, scratchbuilt on Cambrian POA kit underframe parts. AME produce the twisted wire emblem transfers for this and other wagon types used on steel traffic to and from Tremorfa Steelworks.

Gunnell Type 3 No.DC390582, demonstrating some standardisation of the design. The hopper top is new and designed, as far as possible, to prevent the spent ballast from falling between the wagons. Some do not have the angle plates to protect the brake equipment.

Seemingly identical wagons have small details that set them apart from each other. The wheel is equipped with a brake disc on both sides, and the calliper bracket is clearly visible. The opposite wheel on that axle is not disc fitted, as on some wagons.

CHAPTER SIX
Project: Ballast Wagons from Ready to Run Models

Despite their unprepossessing title, ballast wagons offer something a bit out of the ordinary and this chapter will touch on some of their more appealing aspects. The two rtr models chosen for this chapter are the Lima Seacow bogie ballast hopper and the Lima PGA aggregate hopper wagon, both easily obtained new or second-hand. The first is subject to a rebuild into the 1981 design of the Seacow 40t ballast hopper with new bogies, hopper detail and a repaint. The second sees considerably more in the way of surgery - extensive rebuilding into one of the variants of the ZFA Gunnell ballast wagon using a simple A1-Railmatch conversion kit.

40t YGB Seacow Ballast Hopper Wagon

Lima produce a version of this wagon in OO scale with bogies of a continental pattern. The simplest way to detail it is to fit a set of Cambrian Gloucester bogies. If you are modelling a Seacow ballast hopper, TOPS coded YGB, remove the vacuum cylinders because these wagons are

A feature of DC390540 (a Gunnell Type 3 rebuilt from PGA PR14132) is the original hopper top, fitted with substantial end plates to protect the brake gear. Fitted with normal Oleo buffers and instanter couplings.

Gunnell Type 3, DC390540, showing the remains of the end platform.

A typical donor vehicle for the Gunnell programme. This PGA hopper wagon was in revenue service when photographed and gives some idea of the rebuilding work. PR14038 was rebuilt into Gunnell ZFA No.DC390599.

airbraked with a through vacuum pipe. Alternatively, if modelling the Sealion, retain the vacuum cylinders as this vehicle is dual braked with AFI and airbrakes. Vacuum brakes are being eliminated from the operational wagon fleet owned by EWS, so Sealion ballast hoppers are losing their vacuum

AFI equipment and being recoded YGB Seacow as a result.

Newer Seacows, differing structurally from earlier examples, were built at Shildon and Ashford to design code YG500H, TOPS code YGB-A; Y27 type bogies are used instead of standard Gloucester designs. Vertical

bodyside ribs are welded rather than riveted and safety canopies fitted to the end platforms from new, to prevent staff making contact with overhead wires. Only a few of these vehicles have seen any specialised modifications since new, though some have been fitted with generator and

DC 390581, Gunnell Type 2. BSC pedestal suspension units are characteristic of these wagons. This detail is faithfully represented on the Lima PGA model. 1. Triangular ribs 2. Upper panel is reduced in height 3. Angle plates to prevent spillage of ballast 4. TOPS data panel 5. BSC pedestal suspension 6. Air brake pipes 7. Discharge door mechanism 8. Support brackets 9. Unmodified headstocks 10. Oval buffers 11. Brake wheel.

Immaculate Seacows of the 1981 'build', at Tyne Yard in January 1993. DB980019 and 980104 are from Lot 3966 built at Shildon to Diagram YG500H. In addition to the welded construction and Y27 bogies, it is possible to see the lighting equipment to the end platforms. Electrical junction boxes and jumper cables are fitted to the end handrails. They are modified to work with a Stingray ballast hopper wagon. 1. Electrical fittings and connections for 'Sling ray' operation 2. Discharge wheel 3. TOPS data panel 4. Ribs are welded on 1981 builds 5. Platform guard light 6. Platform guard light 7. Access platform 8. Steps 9. Y27 bogie 10. Discharge chute.

lighting equipment for night-time ballasting work. These generator fitted Stingray wagons are operated in rakes of light-fitted Seacow ballast hoppers and are stationed throughout the country.

Modelling

To model a Seacow ballast hopper from the 1980 'build', purchase a set of Appleby Model Engineering (AME) Y27C bogies. A1-Railmatch wagon bogie frames will make assembly of the Y27C bogies a simple affair. On the styrene front, obtain a pack of microstrip measuring 10 by 40thou from Evergreen or Slaters for modifying vertical ribs. A1-Railmatch produce a fine etch for the platform canopy, including see-through mesh common with these parts. Add MJT coupling hooks, Roco air pipes and a cosmetic tail lamp to your shopping list.

Dispose of the vacuum cylinders and original Lima bogies. There are no prototypes to model that have this bogie type, so keeping them is pointless. Cut away the unprototypical dividing panel from the wagon interior by making a series of vertical cuts with a razor saw and then use a sharp scalpel to remove the remnants of plastic.

Cut fourteen pieces of 10 by 14thou styrene strip to 254mm length and apply to the moulded vertical rib

channel with Mek Pak. Turning the wagon over, fit rectangles of 20thou styrene measuring 10mm by 10 mm over the bogie pivot holes. Once set, drill 2mm diameter holes into each to create new pivot holes. Tap a 15mm length of 8BA studding to the holes to provide a mounting pivot for the bogies.

The Y27C bogie kit may be assembled according to the instructions supplied by AME. (The A1-Railmatch etched brass wagon bogie frame is my preferred option - see Chapter 2.) The separate axlebox detail parts provided in the bogie kit are soldered into the axleholes and the back of the sideframes filed to a flat surface, ready for soldering to the etched bogie frame. Standard Kean-Maygib top hat bearings and wheels are easily dropped into place. Any adjustments are made by gently twisting the brass etch until all four wheels sit square on the track. The new, modified, Y27C bogies may now be secured to the wagon with 8BA nuts, using Keen Maygib brass spacer washers for adjusting the ride height from the rail.

Fit turned brass buffers and etched brass safety canopies, using superglue. Add a cast air cylinder to one end of the wagon, located behind the hopper discharge wheel frame. I retain the moulded plastic handrail detail fitted by Lima, for it cannot re-

ally be improved upon. The long legs of the platform roof are glued to the handrails and the short section is folded to match the hopper angle. Superglue has proved to be the best adhesive for small details like these because instant bonding saves time and effort - as long as there is sufficient 'bond area'.

Standard livery of the Seacows is the attractive engineers' yellow grey scheme, with weathering. Some wagons have gained additional lines in yellow or orange, depending on which pool they belong to or, in the case of the Stingrays, an additional horizontal red line. Be aware that the yellow band varies in width, as does the position of TOPS data panels and other lettering blocks. Transrail and Loadhaul repainted some of their wagons into their various liveries. Stingray No.DB980172 was painted in flint grey. A small Transrail logo is applied to the wagon side, providing the only colour in this plain livery. Bogies and solebar are black, the handrails white and cable conduits are painted in safety orange. Loadhaul used their orange and black scheme on many ballast hoppers, but both schemes will be shortlived.

ZFA Gunnell 2 axle Ballast Wagon Prototype Notes

I can only make report, so far as I can,

You could model a rake of Gunnells and not have two wagons the same! DC390504 was rebuilt from PGA PR14002. 1. Top reduced in height otherwise as original wagon 2. Inter-City logo in 'Claret' 3. Remnant of original end platform 4. Brake gear protection plates 5. Air tank 6. Round freight Oleo buffers 7. Reinforced and modified headstocks 8. Steeling cleats 9. Air brake pipes 10. Data panel.

Seacow/Sealion   Statistics

First Builds of Sealion/Seacow Ballast Hoppers

DB982440 to DB982539

Diagram 1/590

YGH Built at Shildon 1971 as Sealions

DB982540 to DB982567

Diagram 1/591

YGB Built at Shildon 1971 as Seacows

DB982568 to DB982927

Diagram 1/590

YGH Built at Shildon 1972/4 as Sealions

Second Builds of Seacow Ballast Hoppers

DB980000 to DB980144

Dia YG500H

YGB Built at Shildon 1981-1982

DB980145 to DB980244

Dia YG500H YGB

Built at Ashford 1981-1982

DB980245 to DB980250

Dia YG500H

YGB Built at Shildon 1982

Notes: Diagram 1/590 Dual Braked Sealion Gross Laden Weight (GLW) of 63 tonnes and Capacity of 40.5 tonnes. Equipped with Gloucester bogies permitting a maximum speed of 60mph.

Diagram 1/591 is the same as 1/590 except for inclusion of through air pipe. Tare is lower because AFI vacuum brake gear is absent. Carrying capacity 41 tonnes; GLW 62 tonnes.

Diagram YG500H is the same as diagram 1/591 except for provision of Y27C bogies and welded construction

on the somewhat tangled story of the ZFA Gunnell ballast hoppers. Numbered in the series DC390502-DC390669, this vehicle type was rebuilt from redundant 2 axle private owner aggregate hoppers during 1993-94. What they also reveal is the lack of a consistent design throughout the fleet;

Gunnell   Statistics

Rebuilt from redundant aggregate hopper wagons into ballast hoppers at Longport, Stoke on Trent.

Design codes ZF001A; ZF001B and ZF002A

TOPS code ZFA

Converted 1993/94

Tare Weight: ZF001A 12.45t. ZF001B 11.95t. ZF002A 13.34t

GLW : ZF001A 50.85t. ZF001B 51.15t. ZF002A 50.95t.

Fishkind Code: Gunnell

Number Sequence: DC 390502-DC 390669

---

some received completely new hopper tops, others retained most of the original features. Variations observed so far have much to do with loading methods, especially when ballast cleaners are used with these wagons. The Gunnells with unmodified hopper tops allowed too much spoil to fall back onto the track during cleaning op-

erations and the extended hopper top was added to prevent this. The general condition of the original wagons as they arrived for modification was not always good, so strengthening ribs were added and the hopper top rebuilt, in order to extend the life of the vehicle. Few Gunnells are exactly the same!

There is a minefield of variations, making photographs an essential ingredient of this project. One of my models is based on the heavily modified DC390588 fitted with new angled hopper top and retaining the brake gear protection plate. No external reinforcing ribs are applied to this vehicle and, extraordinarily, it only received a repaint on the sides. The ends remain weathered with Mendip stone dust. The original raised walkway arrangement is missing. DC390588 was 'rebuilt' from PR14026, a 1973-74 PGA hopper to design code PG006B.

A Donor Wagon for the Gunnell

The donor wagon is the well known PGA aggregate hopper of early 1970s vintage, made redundant from Mendip stone traffic by the introduction of larger bogie box and hopper wagons. Original wagons featured BSC Friction Pedestal suspension, not to be confused with later PGA wagons fitted with Gloucester floating axle suspen-

Gunnell Ballast Hopper Wagon Conversions				
Donor Wagon Statistics				
TOPS Code	*No. Sequence*	*Design Code*	*Builder*	
PGA	*PR8204-PR8253*	*PG002D*	*Standard Wagon*	*1971*
PGA	*PR14000-PR14024*	*PG006A*	*Charles Roberts*	*1972*
PGA	*PR14025-PR14095*	*PG006B*	*Standard Wagon*	*1973/74*
PGA	*PR14096-PR14151*	*PG006A*	*Charles Roberts*	*1975*
PGA	*PR14688-PR14704*	*PG006B*	*Standard Wagon*	*1975*

Note: not all were rebuilt; many were stored or scrapped.

Sealion DB982751 is a Lot 3802 ballast hopper constructed at Shildon in 1972 to Diagram 1/590. Gloucester bogies and riveted side ribs are common to the early examples of this type. Westbury June 1993.

Careful inspection of the builder's plate on DB982804 reveals that this wagon was built at Shildon in 1974 to Lot 3802. It started life as a Sealion but upon refurbishment had the AFI equipment removed. Bogies are Gloucester 2085 FBT5 type. Spean Bridge June 1993.

sion and differing hopper designs as represented by the Hornby model. Number sequences are as follows (bear in mind that a few slipped through the net and were disposed of later): *(see table above)*

Gunnell Modelling

The Lima PGA hopper maybe purchased second-hand and is the base model for all the variants of the ZFA Gunnell. I experienced trouble separating body from underframe moulding, giving up before the model com-

pletely disintegrated. End platform detail was discarded and moulded brake equipment saved for reuse.

By contrast, the conversion to *Gunnell Type* 1. using the simple A1-Railmatch kit is very straightforward and wagons may be completed structurally in a matter of 20 minutes or so. If you have chosen one of the Gunnells with the original hopper top (see photographs) do not use the A1-Railmatch kit or follow the modelling detail for full removal of the hopper outlined next. Skip forward to *Gunnell Type 3*.

A1-Railmatch supply etched brass sides for two variants, ends, brakegear protecting plate, brake wheels and a cover plate for the ends of the wagon to ensure that unsightly holes in the plastic are hidden. Buffers are supplied but if oval buffers are required, then use those produced by MJT. With a razor saw, remove the top 10mm of the original hopper top leaving a lip of 2.5mm for attachment of the new etched sides. Remove the interior dividing panel (unprototypical in PGAs anyway) and clean up any mould lines and flash.

Gunnell Type 1. Select the plain hopper sides from the A1-Railmatch kit and use these in conjunction with the hopper end plates, fitted at an angle to rebuild the hopper top. Retain tie brackets and airpipes located on the model sides. Cut away the end hopper supports, cleaning the model of any mould lines and other moulded detail from the hopper ends. The new hopper sides may be fitted with Araldite or Devcon adhesive, giving time to adjust the parts before they set. The bottom edge of the etch locates at the bottom edge of the original hopper top. Repeat for the other side, before fitting the hopper ends to match the sides.

There is a difference in thickness of the plastic wagon sides and brass hopper top, with a resultant gap between brass ends and the plastic of the wagon. Fill this with a strip of styrene 40thou square and 32mm in length. The external appearance is correct at this junction between the upper and lower hopper. Internal discrepancy is overcome by the fitting of separate hopper pieces inside the wagon, made from 20thou styrene or by loading with ballast.

Install etched cover plates to the end platforms, effectively hiding the locating holes for the end ladders, before fitting the platform guard plates. Guard plate legs are located on the headstocks and the base of the hopper end. New straight hopper support brackets may now be fitted to the hopper ends, using 40thou square

The Sealion is becoming an increasingly rare on BR so the opportunity to photograph a pair was not to be missed. The nearest wagon is DB982497. Built at Shildon in 1971, it has the vacuum cylinders, a dead give-away. This detail is included on the Lima model. Crewe August 1995.

styrene strip. The Gunnells of this pattern are ribbed on the lower hopper side only. Locate the position of the strengthening ribs and fit them

DB982916 with the air cylinder tucked away behind the discharge wheel brackets. The air distributor is immediately visible on the end platform and a plaque on the solebar reminds us of the AFI provision on these wagons. Crewe August 1995

Close up view of DB982916 showing to advantage the bogie and brake detail. Enjoy the rich detail on these wagons, including the network of bolts and rivets. Crewe August 1995.

using 20thou square microstrip styrene cut to lengths of 9mm for the hopper side with two airpipes and 10mm where there is only one airpipe.

Gunnell Type 2. Use all of the etched parts in the A1-Railmatch Gunnell kit, but exchange the hopper sides for the ribbed type. Build the new hopper top as described above with ribbed sides and follow instructions for applying ribs to the lower hopper sides too. Careful examination of the photo-

Getting onto hands and knees to bring this study of the discharge chute and door activating mechanism. Ballast dust coats the side chutes and underframe. Crewe August 1997

graphs reveal that the strengthening ribs on the prototype are triangular in section - impossible to etch in brass, of course. You can live with the compromise, or alternatively, use some fine triangular section styrene and overlay the rib detail. Some Gunnells (of course!) do not feature angled guard plates protecting the platforms and brake cylinders from overflowing ballast, so be observant when using these parts.

Gunnell Type 3. If cutting all of the hopper top from your Lima PGA does not appeal but you want to model one or more Gunnells, then the least complicated prototypes to consider are

those retaining the original, if reduced, hopper top. Some work is necessary to improve the appearance; remove the internal dividing plate, for instance, when taking 4mm off the top of the hopper and dispose of the end walkway and ladder assemblies. The end platforms may be covered by a piece of 20thou plasticard 13mm by 21mm, to cover the holes left as a result of removing the ladders.

As before, refit plastic air tank detail, following up with guard plates made up from 20thou plasticard, fitted to each platform to prevent overflow ballast collecting there. There is variation in the guard plates so use photographs to verify this detail.

Underframe Detailing
There is not that much to say about this area in terms of detailing. Start by paring away some of the excess plastic from the insides of the axleguards and drill them out for 2mm top hat bearings. Replacements must be 12mm wagon disc wheels, equipped with discs brakes on both sides. Be aware that the discs are only fitted to one wheel on each axle, as diagonal opposites.

Careful examination of prototype photographs will show bufferbeams deeper in section than those on the model. Cut two new headstocks from 20thou styrene, measuring 24 by 5mm. Fit these to the model after original detail has been filed off. Then fit tiny linking brackets to the solebars where they meet the headstocks, drill holes for buffers, air hoses, coupling hook and lamp irons.

Gunnells are sometimes missing the gear wheel detail on the hopper door mechanism. If your prototype is such a vehicle, then pare it away with a sharp scalpel blade. Fit either the Lima plastic brake wheel or the etched brass A1-Railmatch detail to the locating hole.

Livery Details
All Gunnells saw some level of repainting, but many parts remained in the original PGA colours, stained with Mendip stone dust. The upper part of the hopper sides and ends are generally painted in post-1984 warning panel yellow. The lower part of the hopper is adorned with spec. 226 Railfreight Grey, including parts of the underframe, which otherwise remains in the traditional black. A few were adorned in Mainline Freight blue.

This scheme is enhanced with black TOPS panels, lettering blocks in white on a black background and a

Materials for Gunnells! A Lima PGA hopper wagon is the donor model for rebuilding into a Gunnell ballast hopper. From top left to bottom left are various etched parts from A1-Railmatch, including alternate sides for rebuilding the hopper top. Also shown are cast oval buffers from MJT and etched brass platform canopies for Seacow ballast hoppers. Modellers interested in superdetailing the Lima and Hornby PGA models may find the etched ladder and walkway detail of interest. This is designed to replace the plastic mouldings shown on the far right.

claret 'Intercity' branding applied to the top of the hopper. When painting your model, pick out the brake wheels and footsteps in white, then finish off with a dusting of dirt and weathering in the corners. Transfers for the Gunnell are nearly the same as those in the Fox Transfers packs for the Lima PGA hopper but modellers will find the general Mainline decal pack from AME of value. Use all of the door locking and repair data lettering blocks provided by Fox in the PGA pack, verifying the locations with photographs. A1-Railmatch supply the simple 'Intercity' branding in their kit, and the TOPS panel may be found in the same PGA pack, suitably modified with black paint and a new set of TOPS code letters. I will confess to extreme laziness when coding some of my wagons, especially if a coat of weathering is in the offing. I will use the closest approximation to the TOPS panel, modifying as few of the codes as I can. I use ready made sets whenever possible and bodge the rest!

Middle and bottom right. Rebuilt Seacow representing the 1981 'build' of this type. The No.5 kadee coupler is not unduly intrusive on this model. Platform canopies are etched in brass, from A1-Railmatch. The model may be improved further by adding etched brake wheel detail and better data panels. The Lima model offers some good detailing projects without breaking the bank.

Left. Example of the Lima Seacow straight out of the box. The central divider in the hopper body and those bogies look terrible. Otherwise, very nice indeed.

Middle left. Work to convert the Lima model into a 1981 build has commenced by replacing the riveted ribs with welded ones, new bogie mounts, new Y27 bogies and pivot screws.

Middle right. The model is painted in Flint Grey for modelling as a Transrail example. The bogies are AME Y27 side frames fitted to A1-Railmatch brass bogie frames.

The model structurally complete.

Right. Donor models for Gunnell Conversions using the A1-Railmatch conversion pack. Any Lima PGA hopper wagon model will do.

Middle right. The top of the hopper needs reducing in height. A line has been cut with a razor saw close to the top edge.

Middle left. The one on the left will be a Gunnell with a simple reduction in the height of the hopper. The one on the right is subject to a full rebuild, with A1-Railmatch parts.

Our pair of Gunnells again. The scars from surgery on the inside of the hopper body may be disguised by a load of ballast. Additional bits are added with triangular section styrene strip. End platforms are fitted with blackening plates to disguise moulded holes and new headstocks are made from styrene sheet. This pair of models is ready for the paintshop.

A first attempt at modelling a Cawoods PFA coal container wagon with small diameter wheels and low floor. I encountered difficulties in finding suitable transfers before AME produced a complete pack of them in October 1997.

Cawoods PFA wagon No.CWD92773 at Swansea Burrows yard. The combination of bright yellow container, red lettering and black underframe makes for a distinctive image. Lots of lettering blocks on the underframe. July 1994.

During the late 1990s, many Cawoods PFAs changed ownership to British Fuels Ltd. Containers are painted red but the wagon itself remained in black. PFA No.BFL92800 is first in a short rake behind 37 717 at Warrington Bank Quay, in July 1997.

CHAPTER SEVEN
C is for Coal

Coal is a very traditional traffic for the railways, reaching if not a peak, than at least some form of stable plateau, with the seemingly unassailable level of MGR workings from colliery to power station in the 1970s. Domestic coal traffic declined to the point of extinction during the 1980s until 'Enterprise' services reversed the trend in the mid-1990s. Export coal succumbed to harsh economic realities too, road haulage in every case being the only winner.

Coal traffic patterns are constantly changing; witness the developments surrounding National Power's rail operations; the 'dash for gas' which cannot keep up with increasing power demand and the privatisation of British Coal. All this and changing attitudes towards the environment all add to the flux.

A general reversal in the decline of coal on the railway is now evident, with new contracts for industrial and short term power station flows. EWS Enterprise is snatching traffic from the roads, particularly domestic coal to Scotland. Traffic pattern changes are mirrored in wagon utilisation, with the continued development of the 2 axle MEA box wagons and re-use of 2 axle low floor container wagons for domestic fuels by British Fuels Ltd (BFL). There is plenty for the modeller to recreate without difficulty.

Modelling Options
1. Hornby produce a standard MGR wagon (TOPS HAA) which offers excel-

lent prospects for enhancement or conversion. The simplest conversion involves the addition of hopper canopies to create an MGR (TOPS HFA). Modellers with a leaning to china clay or industrial lime operations will be aware of the potential rebuilding of the MGR model to a covered hopper wagon.

AME produce an accurate underframe kit cast in white metal which fits the Hornby model. This is the

British Fuels Ltd red paint is available from AME so it is possible to replicate this livery on the AME kit. Rakes of PFAs can be quite short; this train was only eight wagons in length. Warrington Bank July 1997.

ultimate enhancement, offering an economical option if combined with spare hoppers and cradles. There are small detail differences between the underframes of the various lime hoppers and variants of the basic MGR wagon design.

2. The Bachmann model of the one-time common domestic coal hopper wagon (TOPS HEA) is highly acclaimed for its superb detail and finish. This prototype was also produced by Dapol Model Railways at one time, with very

little to tell between the two versions. The underframe is used by Bachmann for their MEA 2 axle box mineral wagon.

3. Until recently, scratchbuilding was the only way to model a former Cawoods 2 axle low floor container wagon (TOPS PFA). AME offer a comprehensive kit for this prototype, supported by excellent transfers. The prototype runs on small wheels to accommodate a low floor, making life interesting for modellers and manufacturer

To help with assembly of the superb AME MGR underframe kit, a bird's eye view of the underframe discharge levers. MGR coal hopper TOPS HAA photographed at Toton August 1995.

alike. The PFA was initially used on export coal between South Wales, Lynemouth near Cambois and Ellesmere Port. In the late 1990s, they find employment in the north of England and Scotland, carrying domestic coal in BFL liveried containers. A recent development is the use of this wagon type to carry British Gypsum containers to and from Kirby Thore.

4. A1-Railmatch produce a kit for another design of 2 axle low floor container wagon. This batch of PFAs were operated by Kelley's of South Wales. Restricted to an export coal circuit to and from Swansea docks, they fell out of use in early 1990. Following a period in storage at Swansea Burrows yard, they were acquired by the MOD for general containers. The A1 Railmatch PFA kit is etched in brass and offered as a budget kit for further enhancement. Containers are left to the modeller to choose.

5. Former SAA steel wagons (400000 series) were converted to conflat P (TOPS FPA) for containerised coal traffic. The Russells operation involved the onward distribution of domestic coal from several Scottish depots by road, after a trunk haul by rail. All of the FPA wagons are concentrated in South Wales for a variety of flows. A problem with broken springs and a limit to a maximum 45mph make these wagons unpopular with EWS for long distance flows. Traffic includes anthracite duff (a coal by-product) to Immingham and (occasionally) domestic coal to West Drayton. AME produce two kits for the FPA wagon; one with the early container and one with the recent aluminium container. A standard ex-SAA 20ft.9in. underframe modified with container adapters is the basis for both kits; see Chapter 2 for modelling information.

Models

The various kits and bits for modelling wagons used on coal traffic are readily available direct from the trade (in the case of AME) and also most retailers. I have chosen both container wagons and MGR hopper wagons to demonstrate the underframes and superstructure modelling. There is something for every modeller, from a short rake of containers to a block rake of MGR wagons.

Middle. MEA box mineral wagon No.391366 is one of the latest builds of MEA for EWS. This wagon type is constructed on the recovered underframes from redundant HEA hopper wagons. Bachmann produce an excellent rtr version. Railmatch do the EWS paint colours and AME the correct transfers. Merehead October 1997.

Right. MEA No.391374 stands in the sun with just a slight dusting of stone dirt. MEAs find themselves on almost any mineral traffic including stone, coal and anthracite duff. Grab unloading is increasingly popular place of hopper discharge. Merehead October 1997.

Axleguard and suspension detail on new MEA box mineral wagon. This arrangement is the same as that on the HEA domestic coal hoppers, a type fast disappearing. Merehead October 1997.

Left. Side view of the axleguard and disc brake assembly of HAA hopper No.352828, at Knottingley in May 1994. The opposite wheel is fitted with clasp brakes.

Right. Extra detail which may be added to the interior of the Hornby MGR hopper body. This depends on how enthusiastic you are about running empty wagons. Note how the underframe tapers towards the headstocks. Toton November 1994.

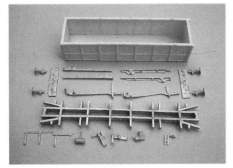

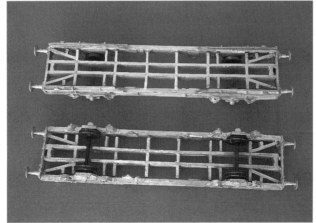

Parts for a Russell FPA container flat wagon laid out for examination. The underframe is the same as that used under the VAA/VBA/VCA airbraked vans. The container is cast in resin; simply wash in warm water to remove casting impurities and trim off the feed pipes. Underframe parts must be cleaned of flash, burnished with a fibreglass pencil and assembled with 70 degree low melt solder.

Fully assembled underframes reveals how they go together. The gaps between inner frame and solebars are easily filled with solder or filler. The container, once fitted, hides them anyway. For assembly work, clip in spare wheels as 'work wheels'. They may be replaced with running wheels after painting. This is not possible with some underframe kits such as the Cawoods PFA wagon.

Looking underneath after the model is complete. Wheels are by Ultrascale, fitted with MJT etched brake discs.

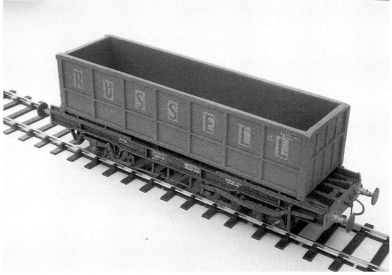

FPA kits take about two hours to assemble, several days to finish with paint and transfers. All of the transfers for both types of Russell containers are available from AME. The delicate cast metal buffers may be replaced with A1-Railmatch turned brass freight Oleo buffers.

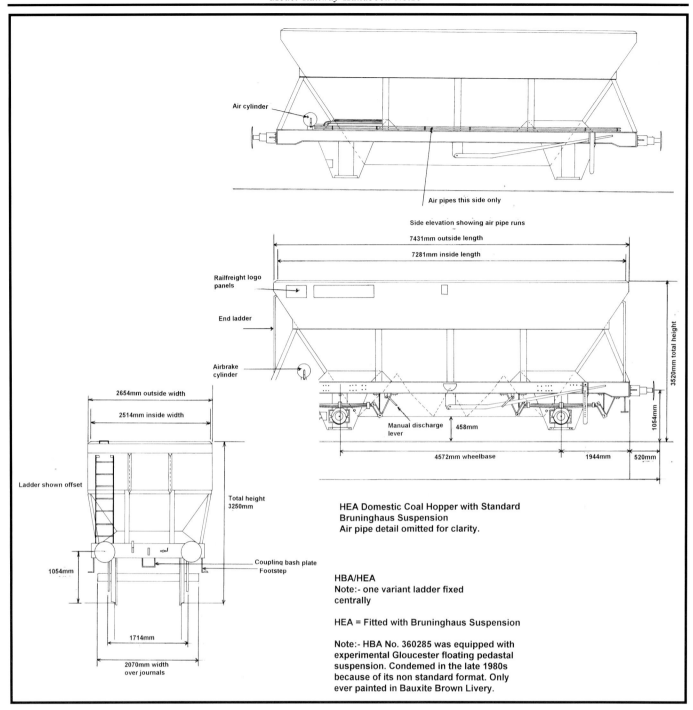

Air cylinder

Air pipes this side only

Side elevation showing air pipe runs

7431mm outside length

7281mm inside length

Railfreight logo panels

End ladder

Airbrake cylinder

3520mm total height

1054mm

Manual discharge lever

458mm

4572mm wheelbase

1944mm

520mm

2654mm outside width

2514mm inside width

Ladder shown offset

Total height 3250mm

1054mm

Coupling bash plate
Footstep

1714mm

2070mm width over journals

HEA Domestic Coal Hopper with Standard
Bruninghaus Suspension
Air pipe detail omitted for clarity.

HBA/HEA
Note:- one variant ladder fixed
centrally

HEA = Fitted with Bruninghaus Suspension

Note:- HBA No. 360285 was equipped with
experimental Gloucester floating pedastal
suspension. Condemed in the late 1980s
because of its non standard format. Only
ever painted in Bauxite Brown Livery.

Unpainted FPA with
later version of the
Russells container. I
have still to add brake
levers and detail to the
underframe.

Both types of container on complete wagons.

A Hornby MGR model as supplied off the shelf. The underframe is not bad and may be detailed by removing the pivoting axleguards. Alternatively, replace it with an underframe kit from AME. Cradle and hopper are exquisite, and may be detailed and changed to various types.

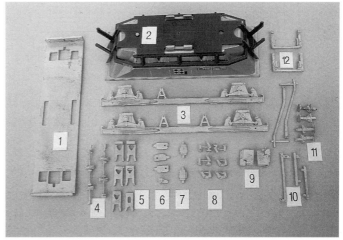

Spare hoppers and cradles may be obtained from various Hornby spares dealers. Laid out are the parts for the AME underframe kit which is designed to accept the Hornby hopper. The cast detail is wonderful and the finished article of a good weight for clean running. 1 Underframe floor pan; 2 Hornby hopper and cradle; 3 Solebar and axleguard sub-assemblies; 4 Discharge door operating cranks; 5 Door bump parts; 6 Discharge levers; 7 Door bumps; 8 Door locking devices; 9 Disc brake calliper assemblies; 10 Door bump detail; 11 Buffers; 12 Clasp brake assemblies.

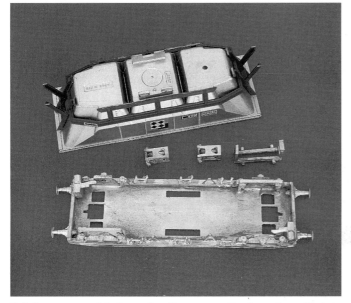

Solebars assembled to the floor pan. Rather than fitting under the floor in the traditional manner, they are soldered to the sides of the floor pan.

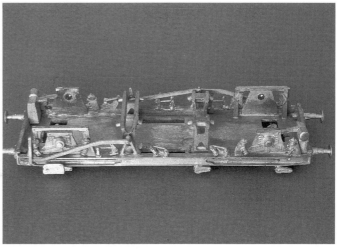

Assembly complete. Ensure that you drill out axleboxes to accept bearings before reaching this stage.

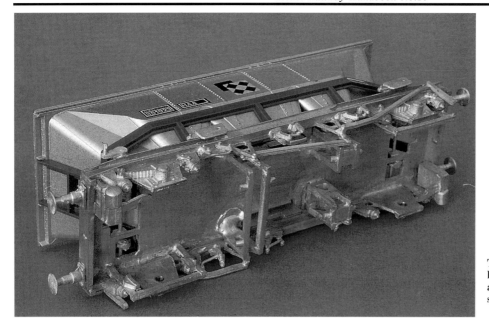

The hopper and cradle clips into slots located in the floor pan. To ease assembly, trim the plastic clips slightly.

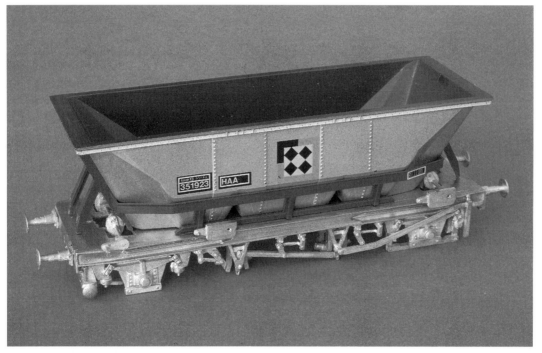

Left. This is looking good. Time to add some detail to the hopper, including canopies for the HFA variant.

Below. The model complete except for decals. A canopy from Parkside Dundas has been added to the top of the hopper. This is quite a convincing model, which benefits from the addition of two cross braces found on the prototype.

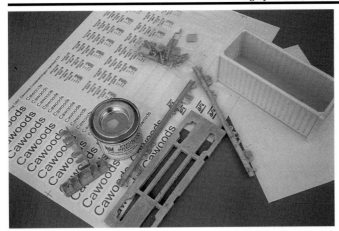

Appleby Model Engineering produce everything you will ever need in order to model a Cawoods PFA wagon, except wheels and couplings. Shown are the transfers, wagon kit and paint. To complete the kit, you need a set of 10mm lowmac disc wheels and instanter couplings.

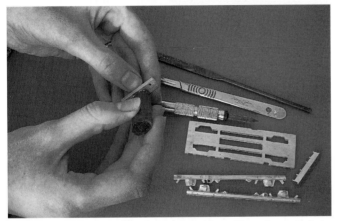

To assist with assembly, burnish with a fibreglass stick to remove casting flash and oxidised dirt.

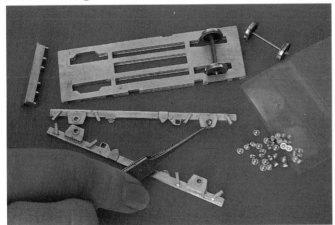

Glue in 2mm top hat bearings.

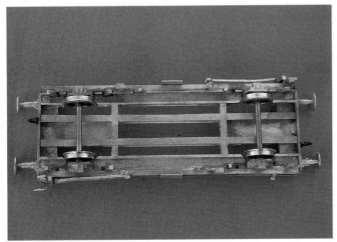

Wagon underframe complete with captive wheels. Protect them from paint with masking tape.

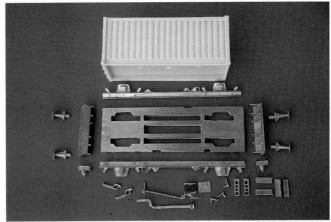

The wagon underframe is assembled in a similar way to the MGR underframe. A floor pan is supplied with solebar/axleguard assemblies. The container is cast in resin which must be cleaned of casting impurities and feed pips.

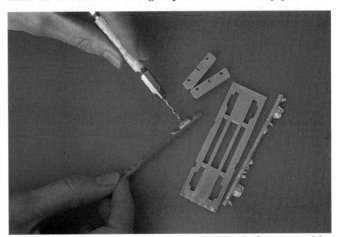

Drill out the axleboxes with a 2mm drill bit before assembly. This job is nearly impossible to do if left until the model is assembled.

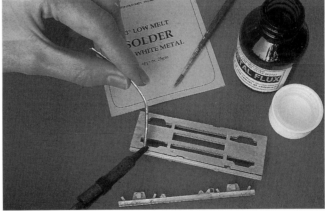

Solebars and floor pan come together in a hiss of hot solder and flux. The solebars are assembled to the side of the floor pan, slots in the floor ensure a good fit. Make sure your wheels are in place at this stage, for clipping them in later is nearly impossible.

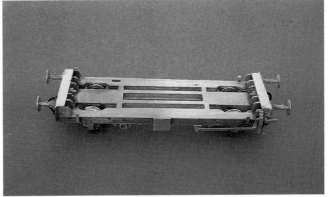

Completed wagon/underframe before fitting the container.

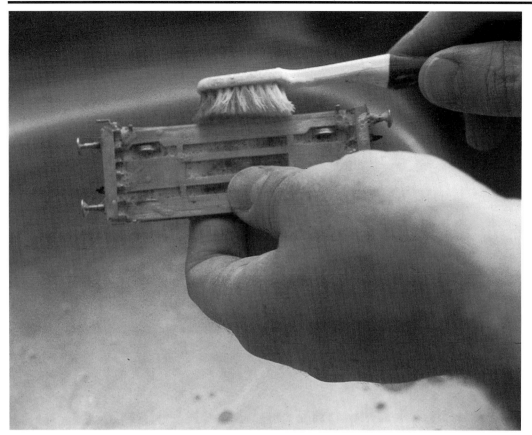

Left. Before priming and painting, give your models a thorough wash to remove traces of solder flux, swarf and dirt. Dry thoroughly by placing the model in a warm place such as an airing cupboard.

Below. One AME Cawoods PFA wagon complete with paint and transfers.

Above. This is a lovely kit, and it finishes well. A small rake of these will look great on even a modest layout. Alternatively, put a few in a mixed rake of wagons.

Below. Before the AME kit emerged, the only way to model them was by scratchbuilding. A pair of scratchbuilt PFA wagons have benefited from Cawoods transfers from AME. Containers are assembled from 40thou machined Evergreen Styrene, the wagon underframes are soldered from brass channel and sheet. Axleguards are etched by A1-Railmatch, intended originally for their Kelleys/MOD PFA container flat wagon kits.

The Tees Yard-Warrington Arpley Enterprise services are a rich hunting ground for a variety of unusual tank wagons. On December 19th 1995, eight CO_2 TTAs were present offering the chance to record STS5324. This wagon was one of the second batch of 31 TTAs, built in France during 1970/71. This particular wagon is ferry fitted but lacks an end platform. The tank also shows the lagging pattern used on this French build, though the ends are more angular. Compare the height of the barrel with the CO_2 TTA behind it and note that the tank on the latter vehicle is slightly lower, betraying its parentage as the Motherwell Bridge and Engine Company.

The grime has not built up too much on this wagon and efforts have been made to clean the dirt from the lettering blocks. Fresh paint has been applied to grab rails, brake levers and axlebox covers. This end is the more bulbous of the two - its opposite will be more conical. We've an ideal candidate from the AME kit in this one! Thornaby December 19th 1995.

CHAPTER EIGHT
Tank Wagons

Tank wagons suitable for detailing and conversion are thin on the ground, to say the least. Modellers are left to make the best of one or two long in the tooth and rather basic models, the Hornby TTA, TEA and the Lima 102t bogie tank. AME has cleaved something of a path by offering a 2 axle carbon dioxide tank wagon kit as well as excellent detailing parts for the Hornby models.

Detailing components from A1-Railmatch and Mendip Models widen the choice of prototypes. This chapter commences with the CO2 tank wagon kit and concludes with the 46t TTA 2 axle tank variants. All of the techniques described here may also be applied to the bogie tanks available from Hornby and Lima.

Profile - STS/Distillers MG Carbon Dioxide TTA Tank Wagons

Carbon dioxide is used in various industrial processes and the manufacture of fizzy drinks. Distillers MG make extensive use of rail to convey such gasses, in a fleet of distinctive TTA 2 axle tank wagons. They may be found in EWS (Transrail) Enterprise services, turning up at Warrington Arpley, Teesside, Willesden, Bescot and Mossend yard for onward distribution.

Our profile starts as far back as 1962 when a small fleet of nineteen 2 axle tank wagons (Nos.STS53200 to STS53218) were built by Motherwell Bridge and Engine Company for the conveyance of carbon dioxide. These vehicles were equipped with airbrakes

and a through vacuum pipe. They had a 15 foot wheelbase, Gloucester pedestal suspension and the large tank lacked any walkways or obvious valves. The first 19 vehicles did not come equipped with ferry fittings, quite unlike the second batch of tank wagons.

The second batch of TTAs (thirty one, numbered STS53219 to STS53249) were designed for CO_2 and imported from Fauvet Girel of France during 1970-71. Not only did these vehicles have ferry lashing points but some sport a prominent end platform too. The end construction of the tank lagging plates was most unusual at the time, but recent refurbishments mean that this feature is all but lost. Some of these tank wagons have distinctly rounded ends with a prominent 'bump' at one end, over the inspection hatch of the actual pressure tank. Others have acquired more angular ends after repairs but cladding plate seams appear in distinctly different places compared to the other batches. Built with a through vacuum pipe on 15 foot wheelbase underframes, these vehicles have lost the vacuum pipes and are no longer utilised on continental work.

The third and final batch arrived in dribs and drabs from France between 1974 and 1978. Numbered STS53265 to STS53283, this is the prototype on which the AME kit is based. A small numbering anomaly crept in with wagons STS53265-276, for as built in 1974 they carried numbers STS53427-438. The tank barrel is slightly larger with this batch, the

ends seem more angular, with larger cladding panels and the seams are in different positions. This batch has cupboard doors to the valve box rather than roller shutters now seen on the first batch from the Motherwell company and the first 31 from France.

The AME Kit

This is a comprehensive kit for the later variant of the Distillers MG/STS carbon dioxide tank; the underframe assembly is supplied as cast white metal parts, including the buffers. All that is left to you is provision of wheels, bearings and couplings. Assembly must be of soldered construction, not a drop of any glue is desirable on this part of the project.

The suspension unit castings supplied are particularly impressive representations of the Gloucester Pedestal type now seen on many modern airbraked vehicles. The detail definition is excellent, on both sides! Beware that there is no room for an axleguard unit to act as a frame, so get everything straight when assembling them to the solebars. This is a freehand job, with a set of spare axles/wheels to act as works wheelsets.

The tank barrel itself is a simple piece of 35mm diameter plastic tube into which cast barrel ends are plugged. The ends differ in pattern on the prototype, so don't be alarmed at the different castings supplied in the kit.

'Optional extras' to enhance the model are a set of turned brass Oleo buffers (stronger than white metal ones); 2mm top hat bearings; MJT cast coupling hooks and a set of 12mm disc wagon wheels.

The order of assembly is determined by the Distillers MG house colours. I deviated from the basic instruction sheet by constructing the wagon as two sub-assemblies, keeping the tank barrel separate from the underframe until painting was complete. The instructions suggest uniting barrel and underframe before adding the side skirts. Painting this structure is more complicated, and it is better to leave final assembly until last.

The Tank Barrel: The cast ends refused to insert neatly into the plastic tube as suggested in the instructions. Instead, paring of excess plastic from the inner lip of the tube is necessary before a comfortable fit is obtained. Drill three venting holes of 2mm diameter into the base area of the barrel. This allows the circulation of air as end castings are fitted and sealed with Devcon epoxy. Make any attempt to fit the end castings without venting holes and pressure builds in the barrel (prototypical but unwelcome), popping your castings back out again!

TTA No.STS53279 is typical of the 1974/8 build, with large tank, heavy duty headstocks, angular ends, the lot. Note the lack of Distilleries MG branding and the Caib logo. Thornaby December 19th 1995.

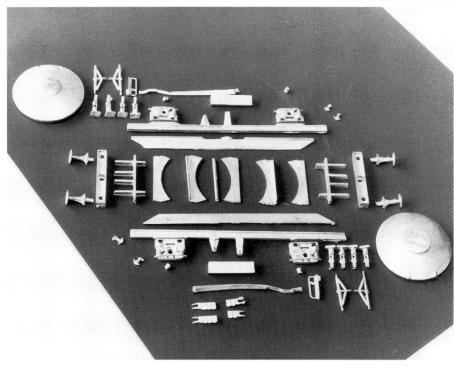

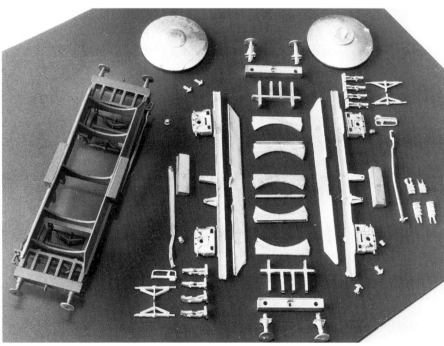

Venting holes will be hidden behind the skirts when assembly is complete. Two of the holes should be tapped with 8BA screws - which will prove useful at the painting stage.

Clean up any excess glue and filler with a file, followed by cleaning with wet 'n' dry paper of 800 grit. Place to one side until the second sub-assembly is complete.

The Underframe: Lowmelt soldering techniques are better than glue to assemble the underframe casings. Before soldering, the parts must be cleaned of flash, burnished with a fibre pencil and given a dry assembly run to check the fit. The solder chosen was 73 degree low melt from Gaugemaster, although an excellent 70 degree solder is available from Carrs.

Begin by fitting the solebars into the recess in the back of the bufferbeam castings, fitting the inner frames to hold everything in place. Swift work with the soldering iron ensures that everything stays in place. Any discrepancies may be adjusted by 'spot desoldering' - melting a little at a time so that minor adjustments can be made, for realignment and squaring up.

Axlebox castings are assembled to the suspension units before drilling out to accept 2mm diameter top hat bearings. Fancy finger work is required to hold a wheel set, two bearings, two suspension units and the underframe and solder all in place, square. And to assemble the first of the running gear, of course... From this you will gather that this assembly stage is by far the trickiest. If, like me, you do not have the ability to grow a third appendage just for modelling jobs like this one, then use Carrs hot tape instead to hold components in place. Accurate alignment of the wheel set and suspension units is critical to prevent a three legged underframe. To cheer you up no end, this little exercise is repeated for the other axle.

From this point, assembly is simple. Proceed with fitting of the tank bearers and check the seating of the tank barrel on the underframe. Two of the bearers have a lip on them for lo-

Top. **AME CO_2 wagon. Lots of heavy metal from Appleby Model Engineering.**

Middle. **Complete underframe of an AME CO_2 tank placed alongside the laid out parts demonstrates how beautifully detailed this model is, with tank bearers, frame detail at each headstock, brake levers, brake rigging and the barrel side plate. Note that the barrel ends are different.**

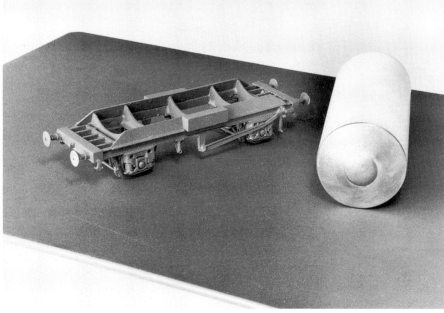

Bottom. **AME CO_2 tank. The chassis and barrel are complete and ready to be united with a touch of superglue. The underframe was of soldered construction, while the barrel was assembled using Milliput filler as an adhesive. The barrel will be painted and detailed with decals before final fitting to the underframe.**

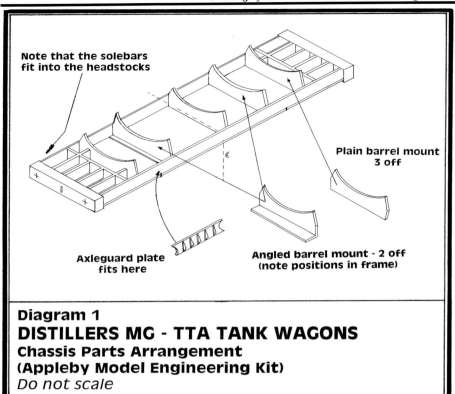

Note that the solebars fit into the headstocks

Plain barrel mount 3 off

Axleguard plate fits here

Angled barrel mount - 2 off (note positions in frame)

Diagram 1
DISTILLERS MG - TTA TANK WAGONS
Chassis Parts Arrangement
(Appleby Model Engineering Kit)
Do not scale

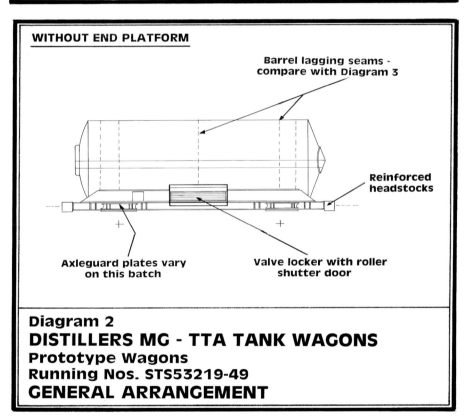

WITHOUT END PLATFORM

Barrel lagging seams - compare with Diagram 3

Reinforced headstocks

Axleguard plates vary on this batch

Valve locker with roller shutter door

Diagram 2
DISTILLERS MG - TTA TANK WAGONS
Prototype Wagons
Running Nos. STS53219-49
GENERAL ARRANGEMENT

cating the brake shoes. Be sure to fit these in the correct locations in the underframe or installation of these brakes is going to be fun.

To further test your soldering skills, fine detailing comes next. Solder into place the eight clasp brake block assemblies with four cross members. The wheels installed previously will aid alignment. Add brake levers and ratchets at the same time, with tiny quantities of solder. Finish off by soldering the MJT coupling hooks and buffers to the holes provided in the bufferbeams and ferry hooks to the side of the bufferbeam.

Dry run the barrel and side skirt assembly to check that no further adjustment of the tank bearers is required. Then solder on the side skirts, checking the barrel fit all the time. Once complete, fit the cupboards which protect the charge/discharge valves and give the assembly a complete clean up to get rid of solder flux, excess solder and any remaining casting flash. A final clean with cream cleaner and a toothbrush will 'shift that stubborn grime', as they say.

Painting and Decals: Railmatch primer is ideal for preparing the underframe and tank ends. A single thin coat, brushed on with care while ensuring that any runs are caught, is sufficient. Leave both sub-assemblies a minimum of 24 hours to allow the primer to harden completely. A cylinder is always a pain to paint all the way round without touching it on any side. The tapped 8BA screws provide a mount to attach a holder made from scrap styrene. Spray the barrel in rail white - two coats may be required for good coverage. The barrel may be held safely until the paint has hardened, then released for masking off the orange line.

The warning line of orange adds a bright splash of colour to the white tank barrel. Note that it is not located midway up the barrel. Careful observation of photographs shows the line lies just below the apex points of the ends.

The underframe is easy to paint, simply load the airbrush with Network South-east dark blue and spray ... all over, under, around. Leave to dry before removing the 'works' wheel sets and fitting the permanent running wheels. Touch in the ferry hooks with yellow; white on the brake levers; blacken the buffers and brake blocks. With the second (and last) use of glue on this model, fit the tank barrel and leave to settle for a day or so. Apply glue only to the bearers so it's nicely hidden away under the barrel. Make sure that you keep the orange line straight and level in relation to the underframe.

Many carbon dioxide TTAs are decorated with Caib brandings in place of STS logos, which is just as well because Fox Transfers only produce the Caib version. Other panels are standard for tank wagons of this type: HAZCHEM panels, TOPS panels, repair panels and instructions regarding loose shunting. Lettering blocks not available include Distillers MG industrial gases and Carbon Dioxide brandings which are quite distinctive. At the time of writing, AME had not finalised the release of their transfers for this prototype, so transfers were found from other sources with, it must be said, limited success.

Enchancing the Hornby 2 axle Tank Wagon
Definitely one of the most enduring models available in ready to run form is the Hornby 45t petroleum tank wagon, now generally TOPS coded TTA. The Hornby model lacks refinement but offers a base for straightforward remodelling and detailing. Its longevity ensures that many are available second-hand at low prices. The overall cost of detailing parts, wheels, couplings and the model itself will not be prohibitive.

A multitude of other vehicles fall into the 2 axle TOPS code TTA/TUA, but these were introduced after the basic 45/46t glw TTA/TTV tank wagons entered traffic and have gross

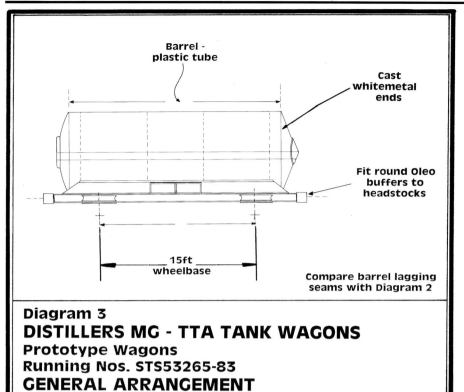

Barrel - plastic tube

Cast whitemetal ends

Fit round Oleo buffers to headstocks

15ft wheelbase

Compare barrel lagging seams with Diagram 2

Diagram 3
DISTILLERS MG - TTA TANK WAGONS
Prototype Wagons
Running Nos. STS53265-83
GENERAL ARRANGEMENT

laden weights up to 51 tonnes. That said, there's no reason why the Hornby TTA cannot be used to model, say, a SUKO 715XX series bitumen tank using available components from Appleby Model Engineering (AME). But - be aware that the underframe and suspension detail for this wagon is very different from the basic Hornby model.

The three basic tank wagon projects described here (Class A, Class B and Bitumen tanks) bring together a number of well executed detailing components from several manufacturers. Any modeller not familiar with the materials used in these parts now has the chance to try them out before moving onto something more complicated.

A Look at the Base Model
The Hornby TTA/TTV has featured in the Hornby catalogue for at least 25 years and remains 'contemporary' from a modern modeller's viewpoint. It breaks down into several parts; the tank barrel moulded in two halves, an underframe moulding and a moulded plastic walkway. In appearance, the Hornby TTA/TTV is a bit coarse and chunky and it has an undeserved reputation for being difficult to rebuild into a convincing form. Overall dimensions, however, are accurate. The barrel measures 97mm on the model, with a diameter of 35mm. These compare well with the prototype measurements of 24ft.6in. (98mm) and 8ft.9in, (35.2mm). The underframe is a one piece moulding with details from the prototype 'as built'. This includes vacuum brakes (TOPS TTV and TTB but without the brake cylinders) and UIC double link suspension. There is no tank discharge pipe detail other than a small disc of plastic, something that the modeller will wish to change. Small details such as clasp brake blocks are coarsely moulded, the buffers need replacing with turned brass ones and brake cylinders of some sort should be added.

Leading dimension are accurate, both the 15 foot (60mm) wheelbase and the 25ft.6in. (102mm) length over headstocks match dimensions from published drawings. When fitted with P4 3 hole disc or plain disc wheels at 12mm diameter, the model's maximum height from the rail is 50.5mm.

The Hornby TTA/TTV is based on a standard Class A or Class B tank wagon in 1960s and 1970s condition. No option for lagged and coiled or bi-

Top left. The AME kit complete, ready for priming and painting. The barrel, consisting of plastic tube and cast metal ends, is not attached to the underframe yet; this will be done when painting is complete.

Bottom left. The model complete, with limited transfers and weathering. The orange line applied to all pressure vessels is difficult to get straight on a model tank in relation to the barrel itself and the underframe.

Middle. Bitumen tanks are very specialised forms of the standard TTA wagon fitted with flame tubes, heating coils and heavy lagging to help keep the bitumen load reasonably fluid when discharging. ESSO61306 is a typical example, photographed at Didcot in October 1996.

Above. As typical as they come. Shell TTA No.SUKO60706 stands at Chester in July 1997. A livery of light grey and red solebar declares it to be a Class A tank wagon.

The AME kit for the CO_2 tank wagon is based on the last design imported from France. The underframe consists of white metal components assembled using low melt solder and fitted with Ultrascale wheels. Because the correct transfers for this kit were not available at the time of building, the transfers are cobbled together from other packs.

tumen tanks has ever been offered by Hornby. Nor has the underframe moulding been updated to include parabolic spring suspension in line with the current active revenue fleet. But never mind, there are ways and means of achieving a model of reasonable authenticity.

What's Available

The last couple of years has seen a number of manufacturers weigh in with excellent components for the Hornby TTA/TTV. A1-Railmatch started the ball rolling with two types of roof walk and ladder arrangement. The use of etched brass allows the fine mesh walkways to be see-through, just like the prototype. However, A1-Railmatch tell me that the more modern grip texture used on roofwalks is not a cross-hatch but a complex shape almost impossible to etch accurately.

Appleby Model Engineering (AME) released their bitumen tank conversion pack soon after the A1-Railmatch offerings, including conical tank ends to replace the dished ends, flame tubes and top vents. Small details suitable for the Hornby TTA/TTV include tank discharge pipes and axlebox covers. If you can get your hands on just the tank barrels, then consider the use of the AME TTA chassis kit.

Mendip Models produce conical tank ends for Class B tanks, which are very useful for other modelling projects too. The ends are cast in metal with a flat edge on one side to match the Hornby tank barrel profile. Mendip are also producing underframe parts useful to convert the Hornby underframe moulding to the more up to date heavy duty axleguard and parabolic spring suspension arrangement.

To Work!

Start by breaking down your purchase of (hopefully) cheap second-hand tank wagons into separate parts. Discard the wheels, tension lock couplings and the plastic roof walks. Decide if the original underframe moulding is acceptable with the UIC double link suspension detail or if you prefer to model the current scene. Contemporary TTAs require a change to parabolic suspension. Superdetailing the underframe mouldings is straightforward enough, for the work is common to most of the 45/46t TTA tank wagons on which the Hornby model is based.

1. Remove, with a razor saw, the buffers, coupling spigots, brake shoes, discharge pipe detail and the strange moulding 'bump' located on the underside of the underframe.

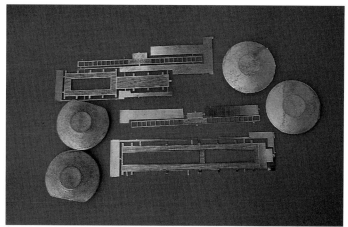

Some basic parts for rebuilding the Hornby TTA tank wagon into something quite different. Cast ends are by Mendip Models, the etched brass walkways by A1-Railmatch.

The combination of different manufacturers' parts have gone a long way to create the two models shown. Those etched walkways from A1-Railmatch look good and may be cut and trimmed to suit the prototype.

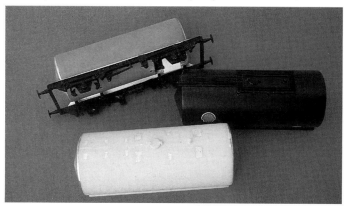

The basic stages of rebuilding the Hornby model. Bottom is the basic tank barrel with holes filled and new conical ends. This is destined to become a Class B tank, lagged and coil fitted. Middle is the same type of conversion fitted with walkways and painted ready for fitting to an underframe. At top: the same idea but using a small diameter barrel cut from 32mm diameter pipe, to model a TTA china clay slurry tank wagon. The underframe is by AME.

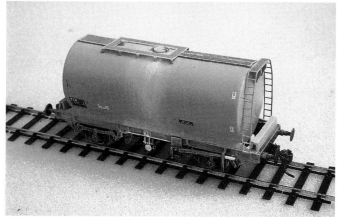

A basic Hornby TTA turned into a china clay slurry tank using cast ends and underframe from AME, walkways from A1-Railmatch and some subtle weathering copied from photographs.

Walkway detail on the same model.

Above. The AME cast metal underframe for the basic TTA design is described in Chapter 2. This photograph shows the parts laid out beside a completed example ready for painting.

One superb conversion kit available from AME is a Bitumen TTA tank wagon. This includes cast ends, chimneys and flame tubes. The model in the foreground has been rebuilt to represent a bitumen tank. The one behind is a Class B tank wagon in Shell livery. Transfers by Fox Transfers.

Conical ends give away the fact that No.SUKO63833 is a lagged and coiled Class B TTA used for heavy oils. The livery is plain black, with only a Shell motif and a sector badge. Roof walk is a 'single' type.

A close up of the Bitumen tank wagon. Hard to believe that this model started out as a Hornby fictitious liveried Texaco model. It retains the original Hornby underframe which is superdetailed. I will replace it with a kit from AME one of these days. Transfers are by 'Lineside Look' and Fox Transfers.

Left. Esso Bitumen tank No.61224, illustrating the weathering characteristic of these vehicles. The pipes at the end and sides are alternative steam pipes for heating coils. Instanter coupling.

2. Drill out the axlebox holes from the inside to a depth of 2.5mm to accept Kean Maygib or Romford top hat bearings. Use a 2mm diameter twist drill fitted to a pin vice and take care not to drill right through the axlebox. Fortunately, the axleguards are far enough apart to allow the fitting of finescale wheels without difficulty. However, no room exists for the installation of an internal compensation unit. If you feel so inclined, it is possible to modify the spring link brackets with 20thou plasticard, to represent the correct pattern.

3. File the bufferbeam flat to remove the mould line and remaining raised detail. The bufferbeam may be deepened as per the prototype by adding a new one of 20thou plasticard with side brackets. Once this is dry, use a 1.5mm diameter twist drill to bore holes to accept turned brass freight Oleo buffers. A centrally drilled 0.8mm diameter hole will accept a cast coupling hook from MJT, adding some detail to the bufferbeam.

4. Many plastic kits from Cambrian Models contain spare parts; the POA/SSA kit providing clasp brake shoes in this case. Install eight to each Hornby TTA chassis with sparing amounts of Mek Pak when the wheels are in place. Accurate alignment with the wheel tread is ensured with some much needed detail definition to the underframe.

5. Add further underframe detail, including tank discharge pipes made up from plastic tube, or use the AME cast part. Brake cylinders for airbrakes or the earlier vacuum brake gear may be fitted to the underside of the underframe, depending on the era you are modelling.

Class A Tanks

The Class A tank requires a minimum of work, and is a good point to start before the more complex prototypes.

1. Start by simply gluing together the two tank halves with a plastic solvent like Mek Pak, leaving the barrel to dry for several hours before proceeding. Fill the roof walk locating holes in the top of the tank barrel with Milliput filler before placing to one side to harden again.

2. File off any excess filler and then use Grade 800 wet and dry paper to smooth off any printed livery details. The same action will tidy up the join between the tank barrel halves to give the appearance of a continuous cylinder. While carrying out this work, care must be taken to avoid damaging any of the filler hatch detail in any way.

Esso operated Bitumen TTA No.61302, marshalled at the rear of a short train at Exeter in 1993. Notable details include the seams in the lagging plates, the cone ends and the top vents.

Headstock detail on No.SUKO67056 - Oleo buffers, instanter couplings, lamp iron and air hose brackets. Note how end of tank is valenced with a sloping plate and the end of the solebar is tapered where it joins the bufferbeam. The heavy duty axleguard and parabolic spring suspension is shown in detail.

Mid-way along No.SUKO67056. Note air cylinder and discharge pipes.

Classic Class A tank; SUKO67056 at Buxton, April 1993.

3. Select the etched brass roofwalk detail for your chosen prototype. Snip the etch from the fret carefully with sharp scissors, taking care to remove any etched tabs with a file. Fold the walkway support tags into place before gluing the whole assembly to the barrel with minute drops of superglue. You could add the access ladders at this stage or leave until final re-assembly. Leave to set before washing the barrel and spraying on a coat of Shell grey paint as an undercoat for the BP livery or as a finish for Shell livery.

Class B Tanks

There are two types of Class B tanks for which the Hornby TTA can serve as 'donor'; those without heating coils or insulation lagging and those with such equipment. There are obvious visual differences between the two.

In the case of a Class B which is not equipped with heating coils or insulating lagging, the modelling work is the same as for a Class A tank wagon described above, except for the livery which is black for both the barrel and underframe. Such tanks carry the heavier petroleum products which have a flash point over 55 degrees centigrade but do not solidify at ambient temperature, permitting discharge of the load without the need to reheat it.

The other class B tanks on the Hornby TTA pattern are lagged and fitted with heating coils to deal with heavy petroleum products which may thicken over extended transport times. Heat applied will swiftly liquidise such materials, permitting them to discharge from the tank wagon. As a rule of thumb, lagged tank wagons generally have conical ends with pipework at one or both ends, associated with the heating coils. A set of Mendip Models cast metal conical tank ends are used as replacements for the dished ends of the Hornby TTA/TTV barrel, though some 46t Class B tanks have a flattened cone profile at the ends.

1. Follow the sequence for a Class A tank wagon outlined above. As before, prepare the barrel with Milliput filler to accept your chosen roofwalk arrangement, but do not fit the roof walks until the conical ends are in place.

2. With a razor saw, carefully cut off the dished tank ends either retaining the small end platform or alternatively, remove that too and fit new end platforms from plasticard when the model is reassembled.

3. From the inside rim of the barrel, pare away any plastic flash which may prevent the cast ends from fitting properly. Always do a dry run to ensure the fit is comfortable.

4. Milliput filler or Araldite may be used as an adhesive to secure your castings, ensuring that any excess is removed before it hardens. This gives an excellent bond and fills irregularities at the same time.

5. Clean up any excess filler and the join line with grade 800 wet and dry paper. Fit the roof walk arrangement of your choice before cleaning the model and making ready for painting in satin black.

Bitumen Tanks

Bitumen tank wagons are a breed apart from the rest of the TTA petroleum types as they are used solely for the transport of this least fluid of all petroleum products. Bitumen tanks are lagged to insulate the contents, which are usually charged into the wagon at high temperatures. Ideally, the journey time should be as short as possible to allow discharge of the hot bitumen without resorting to a second heat application. If delayed, the bitumen can solidify in the tank and it then requires more heat to discharge properly. All bitumen tanks are fitted with flame tubes so burners may be used to apply heat quickly, reducing the discharge time and keeping the bitumen fluid whilst it is pumped into storage vessels.

Further characteristic features are the vents located on the top of the tank barrel, typically four to a wagon in the case of 46t TTAs. These permit the fumes from reheating to escape. AME produce a small conversion kit for the Hornby TTA, including the top vents or chimneys, flames tubes and conical ends which may be used to model many of the 46t TTA bitumen tank wagons. When combined with A1-Railmatch etched brass roofwalk arrangements, the overall effect is very satisfying.

1. With reference to the notes above for preparing a Class B tank with conical ends, fit the AME cast ends and complete all of the other filling and cleaning tasks before proceeding with the fitting of flame tubes and chimneys.

2. AME has cast locating holes in the conical ends for the installation of flame tubes. You may find that some

Modellers interested in advanced tank wagon building techniques can use the available parts to model bogie types too. Shown here are part completed 'Silver Bullets' (as these stainless steel clad tanks are termed) for china clay slurry. Note some slight design differences between them.

of the locating holes require opening out to allow a snug fit. With roof walks in place, locate the chimney, fitting them with small spots of superglue. I felt that the castings for the chimney details were a shade on the large side, and you too may wish to cut them back before fixing into place. In the case of the Hornby TTA, I fitted a double roof walk arrangement to my wagon and fitted the chimneys on the inside of each walkway.

Finishing

The underframe and barrel may be painted separately before joining the two together. The appropriate ladders could be painted separately and fitted using the original plastic spigots on the underframe moulding. Careful observation of prototype photographs will show separate panels for HAZCHEM markings. Generally, they are not applied directly to the tank side of any Shell owned wagons. This panel also conveys warnings regarding the suitability of the vehicle for certain types of load. Small pieces of 20thou plasticard 8mm by 5mm will be large enough to accept both Fox Transfers and Lineside Look HAZCHEM panels.

Take care when choosing wheels for these vehicles. Post-1990 refurbished TTA tank wagons are fitted with plain disc as opposed to 3 hole disc wheels. In the case of Shell Oil TTAs, disc wheel sets are painted pale blue, though it is only noticeable on recently overhauled vehicles. This, and bright yellow axlebox covers, denotes an overhauled vehicle.

Underframe Detailing

A useful cast metal underframe for the Hornby TTA is available from AME. (Kit No.4U04 - see Chapter 2). This may be used with spare tank barrels, available from numerous Hornby dealers (refer to monthly magazines to find out who sells them) so second-hand models are not necessary.

Liveries

As described above, the general tank wagon liveries have remained relatively unchanged, at least until recent times. As a general rule, the barrels of Class A wagons were painted light grey, with the underframe in black and the solebars painted red. Class B and bitumen wagons are plain black, relieved only by the HAZCHEM markings and any owner brandings. Generally, bitumen tanks are not branded at all, with only the fleet numbers in white; product grade numbers are black on orange circles and the HAZCHEM panels are also noticeable (as you'd expect).

As a rule, most companies maintained a livery status quo with respect to the Class A tank wagons, though British Petroleum negotiated with BR in recent years to apply its corporate colours. Permission was granted and the result is a colourful vehicle sporting a green barrel, yellow solebars and black chassis. The BP logo is applied in yellow to the barrel side.

All the livery colours are available from AME, including the BP scheme and Shell grey. Support from transfer manufacturers is excellent with everything from BP to bitumen decals available. It is possible to model virtually all post-1990 TTA prototypes using the Hornby TTA model.

Summary of Vehicle History

Built from 1964 onwards, the 45/46t glw tank wagon was ordered in huge numbers by BP/Shell Mex and many other oil companies to take advantage of the new 22.5t axle loading permitted on certain routes. They replaced many old and obsolete types as BR urged the major oil companies to commit themselves to rail for long term contracts. The design is described as 'monobloc', with the tank barrel set into the wagon frame to allow the use of larger diameter barrels. The underframe is an all steel assembly with a 15ft. wheelbase, vacuum brakes and heavy duty axleguards equipped with UIC double link suspension. From January 1966, all of the 45t tank wagons had to be equipped with airbrakes.

In 1976 the Shell Mex/BP joint distribution arrangement was disbanded with the fleet split 60-40 between the companies. Shell Oil got the lion's share. 1979-1980 saw the conversion to airbrakes of wagons originally built with vacuum braking.

In 1981 The decision was taken to upgrade suspensions for modern operating speeds, with UIC double link suspension replaced by Bruninghaus Parabolic springs. From 1981, any wagons converted to airbrakes were fitted

The angle on depressed centre slurry tanks is only a few degrees. These are two current projects, with examples of cast ends suitable for this type of job. The Y25 fabricated bogie sideframes come from Mendip Models.

with new springs. Most of the vacuum braked revenue fleet was sold or withdrawn from use by 1984. During this time many other wagons had changed hands, such as the Texaco fleet which was sold to E G Steele. Some Shell wagons changed hands too, with Esso acquiring second-hand vehicles. A few Class B lagged and coiled tanks found themselves converted to bitumen tanks.

From 1987 Shell started to apply the company logo. Prior to that, wagons were generally unmarked. Many redundant tank wagons found themselves withdrawn from service and the tank barrel removed. The fully serviceable underframes found reuse under a number of 'new' wagon types including box wagons for South Wales scrap traffic. In 1989 Shell introduced a more complex series of brandings on some of their wagons. In 1990/ 1991 BP introduced its corporate image of green and yellow to its active fleet, breaking the Class A livery rule in the TTA fleet for the first time.

In 1998 the TTA tank wagon on which the Hornby model is taken is still in active service with many operators including Shell, BP, Esso (who hired and purchased several types from Shell MEX/BP) and Mobil Oil. Many TTA vehicles now find themselves used for other purposes, such as solvents and industrial chemicals.

The 45/46t glw tank wagon remains the most common type on our railway system thanks to the huge building programmes of the 1960s. A modeller of current railway practice cannot really get away without a few

'Advanced tank wagon building' can be employed for all manner of 2 axle tanks. This is a model of a former Bitumen 51 tonner, TOPS coded TUA. Some are used for china clay slurry. The model is ready for painting and features a plastic tube as a barrel, cast ends by Mendip Models, a Lima prestflo underframe lengthened with 4mm channel and detailing in styrene strip and card. I am not sure if the filler hatch detail is correct, but once again A1-Railmatch walkways and ladders complete the picture.

at least, even if they are only for fuel oil deliveries to the local traction and rolling stock depots. Such deliveries are still common today, offering modelling opportunities with the Hornby tank without the need to operate large rakes of wagons.

The original Hornby liveries are generally fictitious, but many enthu-

siasts are not aware that the 'Milk Marketing Board' scheme applied to one model was pretty close. The MMB acquired five 46t TTF tank wagons, MMB42866 to MMB42870 for carrying milk. These vehicles were stored until recently, along with the rest of the fleet, in the west country.